Ex libris

Rudyard Kipling

Selected Poems

Portrait of Rudyard Kipling

SELECTED POEMS

Rudyard Kipling

COLLECTOR'S POETRY LIBRARY

This edition first published in 2004 by
COLLECTOR'S POETRY LIBRARY
an imprint of CRW Publishing Limited
69 Gloucester Crescent, London NW1 7EG

ISBN 1 904919 24 3

This edition copyright © CRW Publishing Limited 2004

2 4 6 8 10 9 7 5 3 1

Typeset in Perpetua by Bookcraft Ltd,
Stroud, Gloucestershire, UK

Printed and bound in China by Imago

Contents

Howard Pyle, 'McAndrew and His Engine' (1894)

SCHOOLBOY LYRICS

BY

RUDYARD KIPLING

Schoolboy Lyrics, Kipling's first book

Introduction

RUDYARD Kipling was born in Bombay on 30 December 1865, the son of John Lockwood Kipling, an artist and teacher. His first five years were spent beneath the sun, ingesting the culture and languages of India, and were a blissfully happy time for him. In 1870, however, the boy was sent back to England, to live with a foster family in Southsea, who appear to have mistreated him. This sudden change, from the excitement and bustle of Bombay to the dreariness and conformity of a small English town, had a profound effect on him. He was miserable in Southsea, and longed for the ease and the exoticism of the Empire: a yearning for foreign climes which haunts the majority of his adult writing.

After a period at the United Services College in Westward Ho (which inspired his classic collection of school stories, *Stalky & Co.*), he returned to India at the age of 16, to work as a journalist on the *Civil and Military Gazette*. It was at this time that Kipling began publishing the first of his many hundreds of poems and stories: early works which soon gained him an audience back home. He returned to England in 1889, publishing *Barrack-Room Ballads* to great acclaim, and marrying his American sweetheart Carrie Balestier. A period of travel followed, to the United States and elsewhere, during which he wrote *Captains Courageous* and the two *Jungle* books. Settling again in England (where he was offered, and declined, the Poet Laureateship), Kipling started a family. Sadly, however, two of his children were destined to die before him: his daughter Josephine at the age of six, and his son John (the 'My Boy Jack' of the poem), at the age of eighteen, killed in the Battle of Loos (1915).

Despite these personal tragedies, and an increasingly difficult marriage, Kipling continued to produce a prodigious amount of work, including poems, novels, short stories and journalism, until well into the twentieth century. He refused some further honours (a knighthood in 1899 and the Order of Merit in 1922), and accepted some others (the Nobel Prize for Literature in 1907, and several honorary degrees).

Kipling died in 1936. His ashes were placed in Westminster Abbey, and his autobiography, *Something of Myself*, was published posthumously the same year.

The poems of Rudyard Kipling may seem out of place in our post-Imperial age. They can easily be considered offensive, in terms of modern attitudes towards race and militarism, and their literary merit is questionable. The distaste and disdain evinced by some critics is nothing new. George Orwell, in his famous *Horizon* review of T.S. Eliot's *A Choice of Kipling's Verse* (1942), declared that it 'is no use pretending that Kipling's view of life, as a whole, can be accepted or even forgiven by any civilised person', and went on to discuss Kipling as a 'jingo imperialist' and a Fascist, as well as a writer of bad poetry. Orwell's opinions have been reflected in critical analysis of Kipling ever since. But how fair is this assessment? Is it reasonable that Kipling, as the unofficial laureate of the British Empire, should be derided and condemned as racist and irrelevant? Is it justifiable to dismiss his poetry – all the many thousands of stanzas he published throughout his prolific career – as simply 'bad'?

In defence of Kipling, one can argue several points. Firstly, perhaps, that a high proportion of the distaste felt by Orwell and some of his generation is not for Kipling's poetry itself, or indeed, for Kipling the man, but for the period in history and the political attitudes he represents. Kipling wrote the bulk of his work during the late-Victorian 'golden age' of the British Empire and of British expansionism, and much of it reflects the Imperial concerns of that time. He was born in India (the 'jewel in the crown' of Queen Victoria's empire); he lived there for a good portion of his life; and he wrote a great deal about the Indian Raj and its ways, as well as a great deal about the native Indian way of life and the Indian geography. He also wrote frequently about the military side of the Empire. Although never in the army himself, he seems to have felt a great deal of affection for the British soldier, and many of his poems deal with army life. Sometimes, he writes of specific campaigns in Burma or in South Africa (and later, of course, in the fields of France), but, more usually, he depicts military life as it could be almost anywhere across the Empire. Yet, whatever history may have subsequently decided about the tyrannies and inequities of this period, about the Indian Raj and the British army, one cannot lay the blame for them at their chronicler's door. In the majority of his work, Kipling is merely reflecting the attitudes and the beliefs which were current at the time.

Further to this, however, one can argue that Kipling was not, in fact, an apologist for the Empire; that he does not necessarily believe the things he is saying. If one reads his output carefully, remembering that many of his poems are written from the point of view of a narrator who is clearly not Kipling himself, it becomes apparent that the poet does not invariably side with the establishment or the upper class. Part of the reason for his great popularity is that Kipling was, in many ways, the poet of the common man. His military verses rarely give the point of view of the officer class, but speak instead of the junior ranks: the privates, the subalterns, the sergeants. Similarly, his Indian poems, and those in which he speaks of other nationalities, show a great deal of understanding and admiration for the non-British way of life; and, indeed, celebrate those who approach other cultures with an open and accepting mind. While some may see this so-called 'respect' as essentially patronising, it does go some way to refuting the claim that Kipling was simply an ignorant racist.

Some of Kipling's reputation as a 'bad' poet can be traced back to the political dissatisfaction with his work discussed above. The rest, perhaps, has its roots in Kipling's decidedly down-to-earth outlook. He is not a literary poet, unlike many of his contemporaries in the Victorian and Edwardian eras. He writes essentially memorable verse, designed to rouse or encourage the common reader, or to produce a smile; and while this directness of approach may not appeal wholeheartedly to the critical establishment, it continues to endear him to the public. And although Kipling scores the same number of hits and misses as most other writers who have produced a large volume of work, a great many of his poems – 'If', 'Gunga Din', 'The Female of the Species', and others – perennially make their way into lists of favourite poems, and are eminently quotable. So, even if he may have fallen out of favour with the critics, Rudyard Kipling is still a firm favourite with the readers – which, for a supposedly 'bad' poet who died a lifetime ago, is no small feat.

Peter Harness

Bateman's, in Sussex, where Kipling lived
from 1902 until his death in 1936

Page from the second edition of *The Vampire*
(1898), with an annotation by Kipling

Selected Poems

Rudyard Kipling

*Words are, of course, the most
powerful drug used by mankind.*

Rudyard Kipling

GETHSEMANE

1914–18

THE Garden called Gethsemane
   In Picardy it was,
And there the people came to see
   The English soldiers pass.
We used to pass – we used to pass
   Or halt, as it might be,
And ship our masks in case of gas
   Beyond Gethsemane.

The Garden called Gethsemane.
   It held a pretty lass,
But all the time she talked to me
   I prayed my cup might pass.
The officer sat on the chair,
   The men lay on the grass,
And all the time we halted there
   I prayed my cup might pass.

It didn't pass – it didn't pass –
   It didn't pass from me.
I drank it when we met the gas
   Beyond Gethsemane!

La Nuit Blanche

A much-discerning Public hold
The Singer generally sings
Of personal and private things,
And prints and sells his past for gold.

Whatever I may here disclaim,
The very clever folk I sing to
Will most indubitably cling to
Their pet delusion, just the same.

I HAD seen, as dawn was breaking
   And I staggered to my rest,
Tara Devi softly shaking
   From the Cart Road to the crest.
I had seen the spurs of Jakko
   Heave and quiver, swell and sink.
Was it Earthquake or tobacco,
   Day of Doom or Night of Drink?

In the full, fresh fragrant morning
   I observed a camel crawl,
Laws of gravitation scorning,
   On the ceiling and the wall.
Then I watched a fender walking,
   And I heard grey leeches sing,
And a red-hot monkey talking
   Did not seem the proper thing.

Then a Creature, skinned and crimson,
    Ran about the floor and cried,
And they said I had the 'jims' on,
    And they dosed me with bromide,
And they locked me in my bedroom –
    Me and one wee Blood-Red Mouse –
Though I said: – 'To give my head room
    'You had best unroof the house.'

But my words were all unheeded,
    Though I told the grave MD.
That the treatment really needed
    Was a dip in open sea
That was lapping just below me,
    Smooth as silver, white as snow –
And it took three men to throw me
    When I found I could not go.

Half the night I watched the Heavens
    Fizz like '81 champagne –
Fly to sixes and to sevens,
    Wheel and thunder back again;
And when all was peace and order
    Save one planet nailed askew,
Much I wept because my warder
    Would not let me set it true.

After frenzied hours of waiting,
    When the Earth and Skies were dumb,
Pealed an awful voice dictating
    An interminable sum,
Changing to a tangled story –
    'What she said you said I said –'
Till the Moon arose in glory,
    And I found her … in my head;

Then a Face came, blind and weeping,
    And It couldn't wipe Its eyes,
And It muttered I was keeping
    Back the moonlight from the skies;
So I patted It for pity,
    But It whistled shrill with wrath,
And a huge, black Devil City
    Poured its peoples on my path.

So I fled with steps uncertain
    On a thousand-year-long race,
But the bellying of the curtain
    Kept me always in one place,
While the tumult rose and maddened
    To the roar of Earth on fire,
Ere it ebbed and sank and saddened
    To a whisper tense as wire.

In intolerable stillness
    Rose one little, little star,
And it chuckled at my illness,
    And it mocked me from afar;
And its brethren came and eyed me,
    Called the Universe to aid,
Till I lay, with naught to hide me,
    'Neath the Scorn of All Things Made.

Dun and saffron, robed and splendid
    Broke the solemn, pitying Day,
And I knew my pains were ended,
    And I turned and tried to pray;
But my speech was shattered wholly,
    And I wept as children weep,
Till the dawn-wind, softly, slowly,
    Brought to burning eyelids sleep.

SESTINA OF THE TRAMP-ROYAL

SPEAKIN' in general, I 'ave tried 'em all –
The 'appy roads that take you o'er the world.
Speakin' in general, I 'ave found them good
For such as cannot use one bed too long,
But must get 'ence, the same as I 'ave done,
An' go observin' matters till they die.

What do it matter where or 'ow we die,
So long as we've our 'ealth to watch it all –
The different ways that different things are done.
An' men an' women lovin' in this world;
Takin' our chances as they come along,
An' when they ain't, pretendin' they are good?

In cash or credit – no, it aren't no good;
You 'ave to 'ave the 'abit or you'd die,
Unless you lived your life but one day long,
Nor didn't prophesy nor fret at all,
But drew your tucker some'ow from the world,
An' never bothered what you might ha' done.

But, Gawd, what things are they I 'aven't done?
I've turned my 'and to most, an' turned it good,
In various situations round the world –
For 'im that doth not work must surely die;
But that's no reason man should labour all
'Is life on one same shift – life's none so long.

Therefore, from job to job I've moved along.
Pay couldn't 'old me when my time was done,
For something in my 'ead upset it all,
Till I 'ad dropped whatever 'twas for good,
An', out at sea, be'eld the dock-lights die,
An' met my mate – the wind that tramps the world!

It's like a book, I think, this bloomin' world,
Which you can read and care for just so long,
But presently you feel that you will die
Unless you get the page you're readin' done,
An' turn another – likely not so good;
But what you're after is to turn 'em all.

Gawd bless this world! Whatever she 'ath done –
Excep' when awful long – I've found it good.
So write, before I die, ''E liked it all!'

THE POST THAT FITTED

Though tangled and twisted the course of true love,
This ditty explains,
No tangle's so tangled it cannot improve
If the Lover has brains.

E RE the steamer bore him Eastward,
                    Sleary was engaged to marry
An attractive girl at Tunbridge,
                whom he called 'my little Carrie.'
Sleary's pay was very modest; Sleary was the other way.
Who can cook a two-plate dinner
                    on eight poor rupees a day?

Long he pondered o'er the question
                in his scantly furnished quarters –
Then proposed to Minnie Boffkin,
                eldest of Judge Boffkin's daughters.
Certainly an impecunious Subaltern was not a catch,
But the Boffkins knew that Minnie
                mightn't make another match.

So they recognised the business and,
                to feed and clothe the bride,
Got him made a Something Something
                somewhere on the Bombay side.
Anyhow, the billet carried pay enough
                for him to marry –
As the artless Sleary put it: –
                'Just the thing for me and Carrie.'

Did he, therefore, jilt Miss Boffkin –
$\qquad$ impulse of a baser mind?
No! He started epileptic fits of an appalling kind.
[Of his *modus operandi* only this much I could gather: –
'Pears's shaving sticks will give you
$\qquad$ little taste and lots of lather.']

Frequently in public places his affliction used to smite
Sleary with distressing vigour –
$\qquad$ always in the Boffkins' sight.
Ere a week was over Minnie weepingly returned his ring,
Told him his 'unhappy weakness'
$\qquad$ stopped all thought of marrying.

Sleary bore the information with a chastened holy joy, –
Epileptic fits don't matter in Political employ, –
Wired three short words to Carrie –
$\qquad$ took his ticket, packed his kit –
Bade farewell to Minnie Boffkin
$\qquad$ in one last, long, lingering fit.

Four weeks later, Carrie Sleary read –
$\qquad$ and laughed until she wept –
Mrs Boffkin's warning letter
$\qquad$ on the 'wretched epilept.' …
Year by year, in pious patience, vengeful Mrs Boffkin sits
Waiting for the Sleary babies to develop Sleary's fits.

MY RIVAL

I GO to concert, party, ball —
　　What profit is in these?
I sit alone against the wall
　　And strive to look at ease.
The incense that is mine by right
　　They burn before Her shrine;
And that's because I'm seventeen
　　And she is forty-nine.

I cannot check my girlish blush,
　　My colour comes and goes.
I redden to my fingertips,
　　And sometimes to my nose.
But She is white where white should be,
　　And red where red should shine.
The blush that flies at seventeen
　　Is fixed at forty-nine.

I wish I had her constant cheek:
　　I wish that I could sing
All sorts of funny little songs,
　　Not quite the proper thing.
I'm very *gauche* and very shy,
　　Her jokes aren't in my line;
And, worst of all, I'm seventeen
　　While She is forty-nine.

The young men come, the young men go,
　　Each pink and white and neat,
She's older than their mothers, but
　　They grovel at Her feet.

They walk beside Her *'rickshaw*-wheels —
  None ever walk by mine;
And that's because I'm seventeen
  And She is forty-nine.

She rides with half a dozen men
  (She calls them 'boys' and 'mashes'),
I trot along the Mall alone;
  My prettiest frocks and sashes
Don't help to fill my programme-card,
  And vainly I repine
From ten to two A.M. Ah me!
  Would I were forty-nine.

She calls me 'darling', 'pet', and 'dear',
  And 'sweet retiring maid.'
I'm always at the back, I know —
  She puts me in the shade.
She introduces me to men —
  'Cast' lovers, I opine;
For sixty takes to seventeen,
  Nineteen to forty-nine.

But even She must older grow
  And end Her dancing days,
She can't go on for ever so
  At concerts, balls, and plays.
One ray of priceless hope I see
  Before my footsteps shine;
Just think, that She'll be eighty-one
  When I am forty-nine!

THE SONG OF THE BANJO

Y ou couldn't pack a Broadwood half a mile –
   You mustn't leave a fiddle in the damp –
You couldn't raft an organ up the Nile,
   And play it in an Equatorial swamp.
I travel with the cooking-pots and pails –
   I'm sandwiched 'tween the coffee and the pork –
And when the dusty column checks and tails,
   You should hear me spur the rearguard to a walk!

      With my '*Pilly-willy-winky-winky-popp!*'
         [Oh, it's any tune that comes into my head!]
      So I keep 'em moving forward till they drop;
         So I play 'em up to water and to bed.

In the silence of the camp before the fight,
   When it's good to make your will and say your prayer,
You can hear my *strumpty-tumpty* overnight,
   Explaining ten to one was always fair.
I'm the Prophet of the Utterly Absurd,
   Of the Patently Impossible and Vain –
And when the Thing that Couldn't has occurred,
   Give me time to change my leg and go again.

      With my '*Tumpa-tumpa-tumpa-tumpa-tump!*'
         In the desert where the dung-fed
                              camp-smoke curled.
      There was never voice before us
                        till I led our lonely chorus,
         I – the war-drum of the White Man
                              round the world!

By the bitter road the Younger Son must tread,
   Ere he win to hearth and saddle of his own, –
'Mid the riot of the shearers at the shed,
   In the silence of the herder's hut alone –
In the twilight, on a bucket upside down,
   Hear me babble what the weakest won't confess –
I am Memory and Torment – I am Town!
   I am all that ever went with evening dress!

     With my '*Tunka-tunka-tunka-tunka-tunk!*'
      [So the lights – the London Lights –
                grow near and plain!]
     So I rowel 'em afresh towards
              the Devil and the Flesh,
      Till I bring my broken rankers home again.

In desire of many marvels over sea,
   Where the new-raised tropic city sweats and roars,
I have sailed with Young Ulysses from the quay
   Till the anchor rumbled down on stranger shores.
He is blooded to the open and the sky,
   He is taken in a snare that shall not fail,
He shall hear me singing strongly, till he die,
   Like the shouting of a backstay in a gale.

     With my '*Hya! Heeya! Heeya! Hullah! Haul!*'
      [Oh, the green that thunders aft along the deck!]
     Are you sick o' towns and men?
              You must sign and sail again,
     For it's 'Johnny Bowlegs,
           pack your kit and trek!'

Through the gorge that gives the stars at noonday clear –
    Up the pass that packs the scud beneath our wheel –
Round the bluff that sinks her thousand fathom sheer –
    Down the valley with our guttering brakes asqueal:
Where the trestle groans and quivers in the snow,
    Where the many-shedded levels loop and twine,
Hear me lead my reckless children from below
    Till we sing the Song of Roland to the pine!

        With my '*Tinka-tinka—tinka-tinka-tink!*'
            [Oh, the axe has cleared the mountain,

                                croup and crest!]
            And we ride the iron stallions down to drink,
                Through the canons to the waters of the West!

And the tunes that mean so much to you alone –
    Common tunes that make you choke

                                and blow your nose –
Vulgar tunes that bring the laugh that brings the groan –
    I can rip your very heartstrings out with those;
With the feasting, and the folly, and the fun –
    And the lying, and the lusting, and the drink,
And the merry play that drops you, when you're done,
    To the thoughts that burn like irons if you think.

        With my '*Plunka-lunka-lunka-lunka-lunk!*'
            Here's a trifle on account of pleasure past,
            Ere the wit that made you win

                                gives you eyes to see your sin
            And – the heavier repentance at the last!

Let the organ moan her sorrow to the roof –
    I have told the naked stars the Grief of Man!
Let the trumpet snare the foeman to the proof –
    I have known Defeat, and mocked it as we ran!
My bray ye may not alter nor mistake
    When I stand to jeer the fatted Soul of Things,
But the Song of Lost Endeavour that I make,
    Is it hidden in the twanging of the strings?

        With my '*Ta-ra-rara-rara-ra-ra-rrrp!*'
            [Is it naught to you that hear and pass me by?]
        But the word – the word is mine,
                            when the order moves the line
            And the lean, locked ranks
                            go roaring down to die!

The grandam of my grandam was the Lyre –
    [Oh, the blue below the little fisher-huts!]
That the Stealer stooping beachward filled with fire,
    Till she bore my iron head and ringing guts!
By the wisdom of the centuries I speak –
    To the tune of yestermorn I set the truth –
I, the joy of life unquestioned – I, the Greek –
    I, the everlasting Wonder-song of Youth!

        With my '*Tinka-tinka-tinka-tinka-tink!*'
            [What d'ye lack, my noble masters!
                            What d'ye lack?]
        So I draw the world together link by link:
            Yea, from Delos up to Limerick and back!

McAndrew's Hymn

Lord, Thou hast made this world
                below the shadow of a dream,
An', taught by time, I tak' it so –
                    exceptin' always Steam.
From coupler-flange to spindle-guide
                  I see Thy Hand, O God
Predestination in the stride o' yon connectin'-rod.
John Calvin might ha' forged the same –
               enorrmous, certain, slow –
Ay, wrought it in the furnace-flame – *my Institutio*.
I cannot get my sleep tonight;
             old bones are hard to please;
I'll stand the middle watch up here –
             alone wi' God an' these
My engines, after ninety days o' race an' rack an' strain
Through all the seas of all Thy world,
              slam-bangin' home again.
Slam-bang too much – they knock a wee –
           the crosshead-gibs are loose,
But thirty thousand mile o' sea
          has gied them fair excuse …
Fine, clear an' dark – a full-draught breeze,
           wi' Ushant out o' sight,
An' Ferguson relievin' Hay. Old girl, ye'll walk tonight!
His wife's at Plymouth … Seventy – One – Two –
          Three since he began –
Three turns for Mistress Ferguson …
         and who's to blame the man?
There's none at any port for me, by drivin' fast or slow,
Since Elsie Campbell went to Thee, Lord,
           thirty years ago.

(The year the *Sarah Sands* was burned.

     Oh, roads we used to tread,

Fra' Maryhill to Pollokshaws – fra' Govan to Parkhead!)

Not but they're ceevil on the Board.

     Ye'll hear Sir Kenneth say:

'Good mor'n, McAndrew! Back again?

     An' how's your bilge today?'

Miscallin' technicalities but handin' me my chair

To drink Madeira wi' three Earls –

     the auld Fleet Engineer.

That started as a boiler-whelp –

     when steam and he were low.

I mind the time we used to serve a broken pipe wi' tow!

Ten pound was all the pressure then – Eh! Eh! –

     a man wad drive;

An' here, our workin' gauges give one hunder sixty-five!

We're creepin' on wi' each new rig –

     less weight an' larger power;

There'll be the loco-boiler next an' thirty mile an' hour!

Thirty an' more. What I ha' seen

     since ocean-steam began

Leaves me na doot for the machine:

     but what about the man?

The man that counts, wi' all his runs,

     one million mile o' sea:

Four time the span from earth to moon ...

     How far, O Lord, from Thee

That wast beside him night an' day?

     Ye mind my first typhoon?

It scoughed the skipper on his way to jock wi' the saloon.

Three feet were on the stokehold-floor –

     just slappin' to an' fro –

An' cast me on a furnace-door. I have the marks to show.

Marks! I ha' marks o' more than burns –

             deep in my soul an' black,

An' times like this, when things go smooth,

             my wickudness comes back.

The sins o' four an' forty years, all up an' down the seas,

Clack an' repeat like valves half-fed ...

             Forgie's our trespasses!

Nights when I'd come on deck to mark,

             wi' envy in my gaze,

The couples kittlin' in the dark between the funnel-stays;

Years when I raked the Ports wi' pride

             to fill my cup o' wrong –

Judge not, O Lord, my steps aside

             at Gay Street in Hong-Kong!

Blot out the wastrel hours of mine in sin when I abode –

Jane Harrigan's an' Number Nine,

             The Reddick an' Grant Road!

An' waur than all – my crownin' sin –

             rank blasphemy an' wild.

I was not four and twenty then – Ye wadna judge a child?

I'd seen the Tropics first that run –

             new fruit, new smells, new air –

How could I tell – blind-fou wi' sun –

             the Deil was lurkin' there?

By day like playhouse-scenes the shore

             slid past our sleepy eyes;

By night those soft, lasceevious stars

             leered from those velvet skies,

In port (we used no cargo-steam)

             I'd daunder down the streets –

An ijjit grinnin' in a dream – for shells an' parrakeets,

An' walkin'-sticks o' carved bamboo

             an' blowfish stuffed an' dried –

Fillin' my bunk wi' rubbishry the Chief put overside.
Till, off Sambawa Head, Ye mind,
                        I heard a land-breeze ca',
Milk-warm wi' breath o' spice an' bloom:
                              'McAndrew, come awa'!'
Firm, clear an' low – no haste, no hate –
                        the ghostly whisper went,
Just statin' eevidential facts beyon' all argument:
'Your mither's God's a graspin' deil,
                      the shadow o' yoursel',
Got out o' books by meenisters clean daft
                          on Heaven an' Hell.
They mak' him in the Broomielaw,
                    o' Glasgie cold an' dirt,
A jealous, pridefu' fetich, lad, that's only strong to hurt.
Ye'll not go back to Him again an' kiss His red-hot rod,
But come wi' Us' (Now, who were *They*?)
                      'an' know the Leevin' God,
That does not kipper souls for sport or break a life in jest,
But swells the ripenin' cocoanuts
                  an' ripes the woman's breast.'
An' there it stopped – cut off – no more –
                  that quiet, certain voice –
For me, six months o' twenty-four,
                  to leave or take at choice.
'Twas on me like a thunderclap –
              it racked me through an' through –
Temptation past the show o' speech,
                unnameable an' new –
The Sin against the Holy Ghost? ...
                  An' under all, our screw.

That storm blew by but left behind

　　　　　　　　　　her anchor-shiftin' swell.
Thou knowest all my heart an' mind,

　　　　　　　　　　Thou knowest, Lord, I fell –
Third on the *Mary Gloster* then,

　　　　　　　　　　and first that night in Hell!
Yet was Thy Hand beneath my head,

　　　　　　　　　　about my feet Thy Care –
Fra' Deli clear to Torres Strait, the trial o' despair,
But when we touched the Barrier Reef

　　　　　　　　　　Thy answer to my prayer! …
We dared na run that sea by night

　　　　　　　　　　but lay an' held our fire,
An' I was drowsin' on the hatch – sick –

　　　　　　　　　　sick wi' doubt an' tire:
'*Better the sight of eyes that see than wanderin' o' desire!*'
Ye mind that word? Clear as our gongs –

　　　　　　　　　　again, an' once again,
When rippin' down through coral-trash

　　　　　　　　　　ran out our moorin'-chain:
An', by Thy Grace, I had the Light to see my duty plain.
Light on the engine-room – no more –

　　　　　　　　　　bright as our carbons burn.
I've lost it since a thousand times, but never past return!

* * *

Obsairve! Per annum we'll have here
     two thousand souls aboard –
Think not I dare to justify myself before the Lord,
But – average fifteen hunder souls
     safe-borne fra' port to port –
I *am* o' service to my kind. Ye wadna blame the thought?
Maybe they steam from Grace to Wraith –
     to sin by folly led –
It isna mine to judge their path –
     their lives are on my head.
Mine at the last – when all is done
     it all comes back to me,
The fault that leaves six thousand ton a log upon the sea.
We'll tak' one stretch – three weeks an' odd
     by ony road ye steer –
Fra' Cape Town east to Wellington –
     ye need an engineer.
Fail there – ye've time to weld your shaft –
     ay, eat it, ere ye're spoke;
Or make Kerguelen under sail –
     three jiggers burned wi' smoke!
An' home again – the Rio run: it's no child's play to go
Steamin' to bell for fourteen days
     o' snow an' floe an' blow.
The bergs like kelpies overside that girn an' turn an' shift
Whaur, grindin' like the Mills o' God,
     goes by the big South drift.
(Hail, Snow and Ice that praise the Lord.
     I've met them at their work,
An' wished we had anither route or they anither kirk.)

Yon's strain, hard strain, o' head an' hand,
                              for though Thy Power brings
All skill to naught, Ye'll understand
                              a man must think o' things.
Then, at the last, we'll get to port
                              an' hoist their baggage clear –
The passengers, wi' gloves an' canes –
                              an' this is what I'll hear:
'Well, thank ye for a pleasant voyage.
                              The tender's comin' now.'
While I go testin' follower-bolts
                              an' watch the skipper bow.
They've words for every one but me –
                              shake hands wi' half the crew,
Except the dour Scots engineer,
                              the man they never knew.
An' yet I like the wark for all
                              we've dam'-few pickin's here –
No pension, an' the most we'll earn's
                              four hunder pound a year.
Better myself abroad? Maybe. *I'd* sooner starve than sail
Wi' such as call a snifter-rod *ross* …
                              French for nightingale.
Commeesion on my stores? Some do; but I cannot afford
To lie like stewards wi' patty-pans.
                              I'm older than the Board.
A bonus on the coal I save? Ou ay, the Scots are close,
But when I grudge the strength Ye gave
                              I'll grudge their food to *those*.

(There's bricks that I might recommend –
                    an' clink the firebars cruel.
No! Welsh – Wangarti at the worst –
                    an' damn all patent fuel!)
Inventions? Ye must stay in port to mak' a patent pay.
My Deeferential Valve-Gear taught me
                    how that business lay.
I blame no chaps wi' clearer heads
                    for aught they make or sell.
I found that I could not invent an' look to these as well.
So, wrestled wi' Apollyon – Nah! – fretted like a bairn –
But burned the workin'-plans last run,
                    wi' all I hoped to earn.
Ye know how hard an Idol dies,
                    an' what that meant to me –
E'en tak' it for a sacrifice acceptable to Thee …
Below there! Oiler! What's your wark?
                    Ye find it runnin' hard?
Ye needn't swill the cup wi' oil – this isn't the Cunard!
Ye thought? Ye are not paid to think. Go, sweat that off again!
Tck! Tck! It's deeficult to sweer
                    nor tak' The Name in vain!
Men, ay, an' women, call me stern.
                    Wi' these to oversee,
Ye'll note I've little time to burn on social repartee.
The bairns see what their elders miss;
                    they'll hunt me to an' fro,
Till for the sake of – well, a kiss –
                    I tak' 'em down below.

That minds me of our Viscount loon –

               Sir Kenneth's kin – the chap
Wi' Russia-leather tennis-shoon

               an' spar-decked yachtin'cap.
I showed him round last week, o'er all –

               an' at the last says he:
'Mister McAndrew, don't you think

               steam spoils romance at sea?'
Damned ijjit! I'd been doon that morn

               to see what ailed the throws,
Manholin', on my back – the cranks

               three inches off my nose.
Romance! Those first-class passengers

               they like it very well,
Printed an' bound in little books;

               but why don't poets tell?
I'm sick of all their quirks an' turns –

               the loves an' doves they dream –
Lord, send a man like Robbie Burns

               to sing the Song o' Steam!
To match wi' Scotia's noblest speech

               yon orchestra sublime
Whaurto – uplifted like the Just –

               the tail-rods mark the time.
The crank-throws give the double-bass,

               the feed-pump sobs an' heaves,
An' now the main eccentrics start their quarrel

               on the sheaves:

Her time, her own appointed time,
                    the rocking link-head bides,
Till – hear that note? – the rod's return
                    whings glimmerin' through the guides.
They're all awa'! True beat, full power,
                    the clangin' chorus goes
Clear to the tunnel where they sit, my purrin' dynamoes.
Interdependence absolute, foreseen, ordained, decreed,
To work, Ye'll note, at ony tilt an' every rate o' speed.
Fra' skylight-lift to furnace-bars,
                    backed, bolted, braced an' stayed,
An' singin' like the Mornin' Stars
                    for joy that they are made;
While, out o' touch o' vanity,
                    the sweatin' thrust-block says:
'Not unto us the praise, or man – not unto us the praise!'
Now, a' together, hear them lift their lesson –
                    theirs an' mine:
'Law, Orrder, Duty an' Restraint,
                    Obedience, Discipline!'
Mill, forge an' try-pit taught them that
                    when roarin' they arose,
An' whiles I wonder if a soul
                    was gied them wi' the blows.
Oh for a man to weld it then, in one trip-hammer strain,
Till even first-class passengers
                    could tell the meanin' plain!
But no one cares except mysel' that serve an' understand
My seven thousand horsepower here.
                    Eh, Lord! They're grand – they're grand!

Uplift am I? When first in store

           the new-made beasties stood,
Were Ye cast down that breathed the Word

           declarin' all things good?
Not so! O' that warld-liftin' joy no after-fall could vex,
Ye've left a glimmer still to cheer the Man –

           the Arrtifex!
That holds, in spite o' knock and scale,

           o' friction, waste an' slip,
An' by that light – now, mark my word –

           we'll build the Perfect Ship.
I'll never last to judge her lines or take her curve – not I.
But I ha' lived an' I ha' worked.

           Be thanks to Thee, Most High!
An' I ha' done what I ha' done –

           judge Thou if ill or well –
Always Thy Grace preventin' me …

       Losh! Yon's the 'Stand-by' bell.
Pilot so soon? His flare it is. The mornin'-watch is set.
Well, God be thanked, as I was sayin',

           I'm no Pelagian yet.
Now I'll tak' on …

    *'Morrn, Ferguson. Man, have ye ever thought
What your good leddy costs in coal? …*

           I'll burn 'em down to port.

MULHOLLAND'S CONTRACT

THE fear was on the cattle, for the gale was on the sea,
An' the pens broke up on the lower deck
                       an' let the creatures free –
An' the lights went out on the lower deck,
                         an' no one near but me.

I had been singin' to them to keep 'em quiet there,
For the lower deck is the dangerousest,
                       requirin' constant care,
An' give to me as the strongest man,
                   though used to drink and swear.

I seed my chance was certain of bein' horned or trod,
For the lower deck was packed with steers
                     thicker'n peas in a pod,
An' more pens broke at every roll –
                so I made a Contract with God.

An' by the terms of the Contract,
                   as I have read the same,
If He got me to port alive I would exalt His Name,
An' praise His Holy Majesty till further orders came.

He saved me from the cattle an'
                   He saved me from the sea,
For they found me 'tween two drownded ones
               where the roll had landed me –
An' a four-inch crack on top of my head,
                 as crazy as could be.

But that were done by a stanchion,
      an' not by a bullock at all,
An' I lay still for seven weeks convalescing of the fall,
An' readin' the shiny Scripture texts
       in the Seaman's Hospital.

An' I spoke to God of our Contract,
      an' He says to my prayer:
'I never puts on My ministers no more
       than they can bear.
So back you go to the cattle-boats
      an' preach My Gospel there.

'For human life is chancy at any kind of trade,
But most of all, as well you know,
      when the steers are mad-afraid;
So you go back to the cattle-boats
      an' preach 'em as I've said.

'They must quit drinkin' an' swearin',
      they mustn't knife on a blow,
They must quit gamblin' their wages,
      and you must preach it so;
For now those boats are more like Hell
      than anything else I know.'

I didn't want to do it, for I knew what I should get;
An' I wanted to preach Religion,
      handsome an' out of the wet;
But the Word of the Lord were laid on me,
      an' I done what I was set.

I have been smit an' bruised,
                          as warned would be the case,
An' turned my cheek to the smiter
                          exactly as Scripture says;
But, following that, I knocked him down
                          an' led him up to Grace.

An' we have preaching on Sundays
                          whenever the sea is calm,
An' I use no knife or pistol an' I never take no harm;
For the Lord abideth back of me
                          to guide my fighting arm.

An' I sign for four-pound-ten a month
                          and save the money clear,
An' I am in charge of the lower deck,
                          an' I never lose a steer;
An' I believe in Almighty God
                          an' I preach His Gospel here.

The skippers say I'm crazy, but I can prove 'em wrong,
For I am in charge of the lower deck
                          with all that doth belong –
Which they would not give to a lunatic,
                          and the competition so strong!

THE *MARY GLOSTER*

I've paid for your sickest fancies;
        I've humoured your crackedest whim –
Dick, it's your daddy, dying; you've got to listen to him!
Good for a fortnight, am I? The doctor told you? He lied.
I shall go under by morning, and –
        Put that nurse outside.
Never seen death yet, Dickie?
        Well, now is your time to learn,
And you'll wish you held my record
        before it comes to your turn.
Not counting the Line and the Foundry,
        the Yards and the village, too,
I've made myself and a million;
        but I'm damned if I made you.
Master at two-and-twenty,
        and married at twenty-three –
Ten thousand men on the payroll,
        and forty freighters at sea!
Fifty years between 'em, and every year of it fight,
And now I'm Sir Anthony Gloster, dying, a baronite:
For I lunched with his Royal 'Ighness –
        what was it the papers had?
'Not least of our merchant-princes.'
        Dickie, that's me, your dad!
I didn't begin with askings. *I* took my job and I stuck;
I took the chances they wouldn't,
        an' now they're calling it luck.
Lord, what boats I've handled –
        rotten and leaky and old –
Ran 'em, or – opened the bilge-cock,
        precisely as I was told.

Grub that 'ud bind you crazy,
                        and crews that 'ud turn you grey,
And a big fat lump of insurance
                        to cover the risk on the way.
The others they dursn't do it;
                        they said they valued their life
(They've served me since as skippers).
                        I went, and I took my wife.
Over the world I drove 'em, married at twenty-three,
And your mother saving the money
                        and making a man of me.
I was content to be master, but she said
                        there was better behind;
She took the chances I wouldn't,
                        and I followed your mother blind.
She egged me to borrow the money,
                        an' she helped me to clear the loan,
When we bought half-shares in a cheap 'un
                        and hoisted a flag of our own.
Patching and coaling on credit,
                        and living the Lord knew how,
We started the Red Ox freighters –
                        we've eight-and-thirty now.
And those were the days of clippers,
                        and the freights were clipper-freights,
And we knew we were making our fortune,
                        but she died in Macassar Straits –
By the Little Paternosters, as you come
                        to the Union Bank –
And we dropped her in fourteen fathom:
                        I pricked it off where she sank.
Owners we were, full owners,
                        and the boat was christened for her,

And she died in the *Mary Gloster*.

My heart, how young we were!

So I went on a spree round Java

and well-nigh ran her ashore,

But your mother came and warned me

and I wouldn't liquor no more:

Strict I stuck to my business, afraid to stop or I'd think,

Saving the money (she warned me),

and letting the other men drink.

And I met M'Cullough in London

(I'd saved five 'undred then),

And 'tween us we started the Foundry –

three forges and twenty men.

Cheap repairs for the cheap 'uns.

It paid, and the business grew;

For I bought me a steam-lathe patent,

and that was a gold mine too.

'Cheaper to build 'em than buy 'em,' *I* said,

but M'Cullough he shied,

And we wasted a year in talking

before we moved to the Clyde.

And the Lines were all beginning,

and we all of us started fair,

Building our engines like houses

and staying the boilers square.

But M'Cullough 'e wanted cabins

with marble and maple and all,

And Brussels an' Utrecht velvet,

and baths and a Social Hall,

And pipes for closets all over,

and cutting the frames too light,

But M'Cullough he died in the Sixties, and –

Well, I'm dying tonight ...

I knew – *I* knew what was coming,
                 when we bid on the *Byfleet*'s keel –
They piddled and piffled with iron.
                   I'd given my orders for steel!
Steel and the first expansions. It paid, I tell you, it paid,
When we came with our nine-knot freighters
                   and collared the long-run trade!
And they asked me how I did it,
                 and I gave 'em the Scripture text,
'You keep your light so shining
                   a little in front o' the next!'
They copied all they could follow,
                 but they couldn't copy my mind,
And I left 'em sweating and stealing
                   a year and a half behind.
Then came the armour-contracts,
                 but that was M'Cullough's side;
He was always best in the Foundry,
                 but better, perhaps, he died.
I went through his private papers;
                 the notes was plainer than print;
And I'm no fool to finish if a man'll give me a hint.
(I remember his widow was angry.)
                 So I saw what his drawings meant,
And I started the six-inch rollers,
                 and it paid me sixty per cent.
Sixty per cent *with* failures,
                 and more than twice we could do,
And a quarter-million to credit,
                 and I saved it all for you!

I thought – it doesn't matter –

                    you seemed to favour your ma,
But you're nearer forty than thirty,

                    and I know the kind you are.
Harrer an' Trinity College! I ought to ha'

                    sent you to sea –
But I stood you an education, an'

                    what have you done for me?
The things I knew was proper

                    you wouldn't thank me to give,
And the things I knew was rotten

                    you said was the way to live.
For you muddled with books and pictures,

                    an' china an' etchin's an' fans,
And your rooms at college was beastly –

                    more like a whore's than a man's;
Till you married that thin-flanked woman,

                    as white and as stale as a bone,
An' she gave you your social nonsense;

                    but where's that kid o' your own?
I've seen your carriages blocking

                    the half o' the Cromwell Road,
But never the doctor's brougham

                    to help the missus unload.
(So there isn't even a grandchild,

                    an' the Gloster family's done.)
Not like your mother, she isn't.

                    She carried her freight each run.
But they died, the pore little beggars!

                    At sea she had 'em – they died.
Only you, an' you stood it.

                    You haven't stood much beside.

Weak, a liar, and idle, and mean as a collier's whelp
Nosing for scraps in the galley. No help –
                                        my son was no help!
So he gets three 'undred thousand,
                              in trust and the interest paid.
I wouldn't give it you, Dickie –
                            you see, I made it in trade.
You're saved from soiling your fingers,
                              and if you have no child,
It all comes back to the business.
                          'Gad, won't your wife be wild!
Calls and calls in her carriage,
                          her 'andkerchief up to 'er eye:
'Daddy! dear daddy's dyin'!' and doing her best to cry.
Grateful? Oh, yes, I'm grateful,
                        but keep her away from here.
Your mother 'ud never ha' stood 'er,
                        and, anyhow, women are queer ...
There's women will say I've married a second time.
                                              Not quite!
But give pore Aggie a hundred,
                        and tell her your lawyers'll fight.
She was the best o' the boiling –
                        you'll meet her before it ends.
I'm in for a row with the mother –
                        I'll leave you settle my friends.
For a man he must go with a woman,
                        which women don't understand –
Or the sort that say they can see it
                        they aren't the marrying brand.
But I wanted to speak o' your mother
                        that's Lady Gloster still;
I'm going to up and see her, without its hurting the will.

Here! Take your hand off the bell-pull.

                Five thousand's waiting for you,

If you'll only listen a minute, and do as I bid you do.

They'll try to prove me crazy, and, if you bungle,

                                  they can;

And I've only you to trust to!

                    (O God, why ain't it a man?)

There's some waste money on marbles,

                        the same as M'Cullough tried –

Marbles and mausoleums – but I call that sinful pride.

There's some ship bodies for burial –

                we've carried 'em, soldered and packed;

Down in their wills they wrote it,

                and nobody called *them* cracked.

But me – I've too much money, and people might …

                            All my fault:

It come o' hoping for grandsons

                and buying that Wokin' vault …

I'm sick o' the 'ole dam' business.

                  I'm going back where I came.

Dick, you're the son o' my body,

                and you'll take charge o' the same!

I want to lie by your mother, ten thousand mile away,

And they'll want to send me to Woking;

                and that's where you'll earn your pay.

I've thought it out on the quiet,

                the same as it ought to be done –

Quiet, and decent, and proper –

                an' here's your orders, my son.

You know the Line? You don't, though.

                You write to the Board, and tell

Your father's death has upset you

                an' you're goin' to cruise for a spell,

An' you'd like the *Mary Gloster* —
                    I've held her ready for this —
They'll put her in working order
                    and you'll take her out as she is.
Yes, it was money idle when I patched her
                    and laid her aside
(Thank God, I can pay for my fancies!) —
                    the boat where your mother died,
By the Little Paternosters, as you come
                    to the Union Bank,
We dropped her — I think I told you —
                    and I pricked it off where she sank.
['Tiny she looked on the grating — that oily, treacly sea —]
'Hundred and Eighteen East, remember,
                    and South just Three.
Easy bearings to carry — Three South — Three to the dot;
But I gave McAndrew a copy in case of dying — or not.
And so you'll write to McAndrew,
                    he's Chief of the Maori Line;
They'll give him leave, if you ask 'em
                    and say it's business o' mine.
I built three boats for the Maoris,
                    an' very well pleased they were,
An' I've known Mac since the Fifties,
                    and Mac knew me — and her.
After the first stroke warned me
                    I sent him the money to keep
Against the time you'd claim it,
                    committin' your dad to the deep;
For you are the son o' my body,
                    and Mac was my oldest friend,
I've never asked 'im to dinner,
                    but he'll see it out to the end.

Stiff-necked Glasgow beggar!

        I've heard he's prayed for my soul,
But he couldn't lie if you paid him,

        and he'd starve before he stole.
He'll take the *Mary* in ballast –

        you'll find her a lively ship;
And you'll take Sir Anthony Gloster,

        that goes on 'is wedding-trip,
Lashed in our old deck-cabin

        with all three portholes wide,
The kick o' the screw beneath him

        and the round blue seas outside!
Sir Anthony Gloster's carriage –

        our 'ouse-flag flyin' free –
Ten thousand men on the payroll

        and forty freighters at sea!
He made himself and a million,

        but this world is a fleetin' show,
And he'll go to the wife of 'is bosom

        the same as he ought to go –
By the heel of the Paternosters –

        there isn't a chance to mistake –
And Mac'll pay you the money

        as soon as the bubbles break!
Five thousand for six weeks' cruising,

        the staunchest freighter afloat,
And Mac he'll give you your bonus

        the minute I'm out o' the boat!
He'll take you round to Macassar,

        and you'll come back alone;
He knows what I want o' the *Mary* ...

        I'll do what I please with my own.

Your mother 'ud call it wasteful,
>> but I've seven-and-thirty more;
I'll come in my private carriage
>> and bid it wait at the door ...
For my son 'e was never a credit:
>> 'e muddled with books and art,
And 'e lived on Sir Anthony's money
>> and 'e broke Sir Anthony's heart.
There isn't even a grandchild,
>> and the Gloster family's done –
The only one you left me – O mother, the only one!
Harrer and Trinity College – me slavin' early an' late –
An' he thinks I'm dying crazy,
>> and you're in Macassar Strait!
Flesh o' my flesh, my dearie, for ever an' ever amen,
That first stroke come for a warning.
>> I ought to ha' gone to you then.
But – cheap repairs for a cheap 'un –
>> the doctors said I'd do.
Mary, why didn't *you* warn me? I've allus heeded to you,
Excep' – I know – about women;
>> but you are a spirit now;
An', wife, they was only women, and I was a man.
>> That's how.
An' a man 'e must go with a woman,
>> as you *could* not understand;
But I never talked 'em secrets. I paid 'em out o' hand.
Thank Gawd, I can pay for my fancies!
>> Now what's five thousand to me,
For a berth off the Paternosters
>> in the haven where I would be?

I believe in the Resurrection, if I read my Bible plain,
But I wouldn't trust 'em at Wokin';

          we're safer at sea again.
For the heart it shall go with the treasure –

          go down to the sea in ships.
I'm sick of the hired women. I'll kiss my girl on her lips!
I'll be content with my fountain.

          I'll drink from my own well,
And the wife of my youth shall charm me –

          an' the rest can go to Hell!
(Dickie, *he* will, that's certain.)

          I'll lie in our standin'-bed,
An' Mac'll take her in ballast –

          an' she trims best by the head …
Down by the head an' sinkin',

          her fires are drawn and cold,
And the water's splashin' hollow

          on the skin of the empty hold –
Churning an' choking and chuckling,

          quiet and scummy and dark –
Full to her lower hatches and risin' steady. Hark!
That was the after-bulkhead …

          She's flooded from stern to stern …
'Never seen death yet, Dickie? …

          Well, now is your time to learn!

THE DESTROYERS

THE strength of twice three thousand horse
*   That seeks the single goal;*
The line that holds the rending course,
*   The hate that swings the whole:*
The stripped hulls, slinking through the gloom,
*   At gaze and gone again —*
The Brides of Death that wait the groom —
*   The Choosers of the Slain!*

Offshore where sea and skyline blend
    In rain, the daylight dies;
The sullen, shouldering swells attend
    Night and our sacrifice.
Adown the stricken capes no flare —
    No mark on spit or bar, —
Girdled and desperate we dare
    The blindfold game of war.

Nearer the up-flung beams that spell
    The council of our foes;
Clearer the barking guns that tell
    Their scattered flank to close.
Sheer to the trap they crowd their way
    From ports for this unbarred.
Quiet, and count our laden prey,
    The convoy and her guard!

On shoal with scarce a foot below,
    Where rock and islet throng,
Hidden and hushed we watch them throw
    Their anxious lights along.
Not here, not here your danger lies –
    (Stare hard, O hooded eyne!)
Save where the dazed rock-pigeons rise
    The lit cliffs give no sign.

Therefore – to break the rest ye seek,
    The Narrow Seas to clear –
Hark to the siren's whimpering shriek –
    The driven death is here!
Look to your van a league away, –
    What midnight terror stays
The bulk that checks against the spray
    Her crackling tops ablaze?

Hit, and hard hit! The blow went home,
    The muffled, knocking stroke –
The steam that overruns the foam –
    The foam that thins to smoke –
The smoke that clokes the deep aboil –
    The deep that chokes her throes
Till, streaked with ash and sleeked with oil,
    The lukewarm whirlpools close!

A shadow down the sickened wave
    Long since her slayer fled:
But hear their chattering quick-fires rave
    Astern, abeam, ahead!
Panic that shells the drifting spar –
    Loud waste with none to check –
Mad fear that rakes a scornful star
    Or sweeps a consort's deck.

Now, while their silly smoke hangs thick,
    Now ere their wits they find,
Lay in and lance them to the quick –
    Our gallied whales are blind!
Good luck to those that see the end,
    Goodbye to those that drown –
For each his chance as chance shall send –
    And God for all! *Shut down!*

The strength of twice three thousand horse
    That serve the one command;
The hand that heaves the headlong force,
    The hate that backs the hand
The doom-bolt in the darkness freed,
    The mine that splits the main;
The white-hot wake, the 'wildering speed –
    The Choosers of the Slain!

THE LINER SHE'S A LADY

THE Liner she's a lady, an' she never looks nor 'eeds –
The Man-o'-War's 'er 'usband,

an' 'e gives 'er all she needs;
But, oh, the little cargo-boats,

that sail the wet seas roun',
They're just the same as you an' me

a-plyin' up an' down!

Plyin' up an' down, Jenny, 'angin' round the Yard,
All the way by Fratton tram down to Portsmouth 'Ard:
Anythin' for business, an' we're growin' old –
Plyin' up an' down, Jenny, waitin' in the cold!

The Liner she's a lady by the paint upon 'er face,
An' if she meets an accident they count it sore disgrace.
The Man-o'-War's 'er 'usband, and 'e's always 'andy by,
But, oh, the little cargo-boats, they've got to load or die!

The Liner she's a lady, and 'er route is cut an' dried;
The Man-o'-War's 'er 'usband,

an' 'e always keeps beside;
But, oh, the little cargo-boats that 'aven't any man,
They've got to do their business first,

and make the most they can!

The Liner she's a lady, and if a war should come,
The Man-o'-War's 'er 'usband,
      and 'e'd bid 'er stay at home;
But, oh, the little cargo-boats that fill with every tide!
'E'd 'ave to up an' fight for them,
       for they are England's pride.

The Liner she's a lady, but if she wasn't made,
There still would be the cargo-boats
       for 'ome an' foreign trade.
The Man-o'-War's 'er 'usband, but if we wasn't 'ere,
'E wouldn't have to fight at all
       for 'ome an' friends so dear.

 'Ome an' friends so dear, Jenny, 'angin' round the Yard,
 All the way by Fratton tram down to Portsmouth 'Ard;
 Anythin' for business, an' we're growin' old —
 'Ome an' friends so dear, Jenny, waitin' in the cold!

THE SONG OF THE DEAD

*H*EAR now the Song of the Dead —
                    in the North by the torn berg-edges —
They that look still to the Pole,
                    asleep by their hide-stripped sledges.
Song of the Dead in the South —
                    in the sun by their skeleton horses,
Where the warrigal whimpers and bays
                    through the dust of the sere river-courses.

Song of the Dead in the East —
                    in the heat-rotted jungle-hollows,
Where the dog-ape barks in the kloof —
                    in the brake of the buffalo-wallows.
Song of the Dead in the West —
                    in the Barrens, the pass that betrayed them,
Where the wolverine tumbles their packs from the camp
                    and the grave-mound they made them;
    Hear now the Song of the Dead!

I

We were dreamers, dreaming greatly,
                    in the man-stifled town;
We yearned beyond the skyline
                    where the strange roads go down.
Came the Whisper, came the Vision,
                    came the Power with the Need,
Till the Soul that is not man's soul was lent us to lead.

As the deer breaks — as the steer breaks —
                    from the herd where they graze,
In the faith of little children we went on our ways.

Then the wood failed — then the food failed —
                  then the last water dried —
In the faith of little children we lay down and died.
On the sand-drift — on the veldt-side —
                  in the fern-scrub we lay,
That our sons might follow after
                  by the bones on the way.
Follow after — follow after! We have watered the root,
And the bud has come to blossom that ripens for fruit!
Follow after — we are waiting, by the trails that we lost,
For the sounds of many footsteps, for the tread of a host.
Follow after — follow after — for the harvest is sown:
By the bones about the wayside
                  ye shall come to your own!

> *When Drake went down to the Horn*
>   *And England was crowned thereby,*
> *'Twixt seas unhailed and shores unhailed*
>   *Our Lodge — our Lodge was born*
>   *(And England was crowned thereby!)*
>
> *Which never shall close again*
>   *By day nor yet by night,*
> *While man shall take his life to stake*
>   *At risk of shoal or main*
>   *(By day nor yet by night)*
>
> *But standeth even so*
>   *As now we witness here,*
> *While men depart, of joyful heart,*
>   *Adventure for to know*
>   *(As now bear witness here!)*

II

We have fed our sea for a thousand years
    And she calls us, still unfed,
Though there's never a wave of all her waves
    But marks our English dead:
We have strawed our best to the weed's unrest,
    To the shark and the sheering gull.
If blood be the price of admiralty,
    Lord God, we ha' paid in full!

There's never a flood goes shoreward now
    But lifts a keel we manned;
There's never an ebb goes seaward now
    But drops our dead on the sand –
But slinks our dead on the sands forlore,
    From the Ducies to the Swin.
If blood be the price of admiralty,
If blood be the price of admiralty,
    Lord God, we ha' paid it in!

We must feed our sea for a thousand years,
    For that is our doom and pride,
As it was when they sailed with the *Golden Hind*,
    Or the wreck that struck last tide –
Or the wreck that lies on the spouting reef
    Where the ghastly blue-lights flare.
If blood be the price of admiralty,
If blood be the price of admiralty,
If blood be the price of admiralty,
    Lord God, we ha' bought it fair!

THE ABSENT-MINDED BEGGAR

WHEN you've shouted 'Rule Britannia',
    when you've sung 'God save the Queen',
When you've finished killing Kruger
        with your mouth,
Will you kindly drop a shilling in my little tambourine
  For a gentleman in khaki ordered South?
He's an absent-minded beggar,
    and his weaknesses are great –
  But we and Paul must take him as we find him –
He is out on active service, wiping something off a slate –
  And he's left a lot of little things behind him!
Duke's son – cook's son – son of a hundred kings –
  (Fifty thousand horse and foot going to Table Bay!)
Each of 'em doing his country's work
  (and who's to look after their things?)
Pass the hat for your credit's sake,
    and pay – pay – pay!

There are girls he married secret,
      asking no permission to,
  For he knew he wouldn't get it if he did.
There is gas and coals and vittles,
      and the house-rent falling due,
  And it's more than rather likely there's a kid.
There are girls he walked with casual.
      They'll be sorry now he's gone,
  For an absent-minded beggar they will find him,
But it ain't the time for sermons
      with the winter coming on.
  We must help the girl that Tommy's left behind him!

Cook's son – Duke's son – son of a belted Earl –
  · Son of a Lambeth publican – it's all the same today!
Each of 'em doing his country's work
  (and who's to look after the girl?)
Pass the hat for your credit's sake,
        and pay – pay – pay!

There are families by thousands,
                far too proud to beg or speak,
  And they'll put their sticks and bedding up the spout,
And they'll live on half o' nothing,
                paid 'em punctual once a week,
  'Cause the man that earns the wage is ordered out.
He's an absent-minded beggar,
                but he heard his country call,
  And his reg'ment didn't need to send to find him!
He chucked his job and joined it – so the job before us all
  Is to help the home that Tommy's left behind him!
Duke's job – cook's job – gardener, baronet, groom,
  Mews or palace or paper-shop,
                there's someone gone away!
Each of 'em doing his country's work
  (and who's to look after the room?)
Pass the hat for your credit's sake,
        and pay – pay – pay!

Let us manage so as, later, we can look him in the face,
    And tell him — what he'd very much prefer —
That, while he saved the Empire,
                     his employer saved his place,
    And his mates (that's you and me) looked out for *her*.
He's an absent-minded beggar and he may forget it all,
    But we do not want his kiddies to remind him
That we sent 'em to the workhouse
                  while their daddy hammered Paul,
    So we'll help the homes that Tommy left behind him!
Cook's home — Duke's home — home of a millionaire,
    (Fifty thousand horse and foot going to Table Bay!)
Each of 'em doing his country's work
    (and what have you got to spare?)
Pass the hat for your credit's sake,
        and pay — pay — pay!

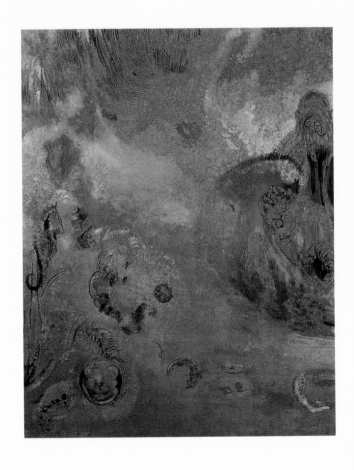

Odilon Redon, 'Underwater Vision' (*c.* 1910)

THE DEEP-SEA CABLES

THE wrecks dissolve above us;
    their dust drops down from afar –
Down to the dark, to the utter dark,
    where the blind white sea-snakes are.
There is no sound, no echo of sound,
    in the deserts of the deep,
Or the great grey level plains of ooze
    where the shell-burred cables creep.

Here in the womb of the world –
    here on the tie-ribs of earth
Words, and the words of men,
    flicker and flutter and beat –
Warning, sorrow, and gain, salutation and mirth –
For a Power troubles the Still
    that has neither voice nor feet.

They have wakened the timeless Things;
    they have killed their father Time;
Joining hands in the gloom,
    a league from the last of the sun.
Hush! Men talk today
    o'er the waste of the ultimate slime,
And new Word runs between:
    whispering, 'Let us be one!'

THE NATIVE-BORN

WE'VE drunk to the Queen – God bless her! –
 We've drunk to our mothers' land;
We've drunk to our English brother,
 (But he does not understand);
We've drunk to the wide creation,
 And the Cross swings low for the morn,
Last toast, and of Obligation,
 A health to the Native-born!

They change their skies above them,
 But not their hearts that roam!
We learned from our wistful mothers
 To call old England 'home';
We read of the English skylark,
 Of the spring in the English lanes,
But we screamed with the painted lories
 As we rode on the dusty plains!

They passed with their old-world legends –
 Their tales of wrong and dearth –
Our fathers held by purchase,
 But we by the right of birth;
Our heart's where they rocked our cradle,
 Our love where we spent our toil,
And our faith and our hope and our honour
 We pledge to our native soil!

I charge you charge your glasses –
　　I charge you drink with me
To the men of the Four New Nations,
　　And the Islands of the Sea –
To the last least lump of coral
　　That none may stand outside,
And our own good pride shall teach us
　　To praise our comrade's pride.

To the hush of the breathless morning
　　On the thin, tin, crackling roofs,
To the haze of the burned back-ranges
　　And the dust of the shoeless hoofs –
To the risk of a death by drowning,
　　To the risk of a death by drouth –
To the men of a million acres,
　　To the Sons of the Golden South!

To the Sons of the Golden South (Stand up!),
　　And the life we live and know,
Let a fellow sing o' the little thingshe cares about,
If a fellow fights for the little things he cares about
　　With the weight of a single blow!

To the smoke of a hundred coasters,
　　To the sheep on a thousand hills,
To the sun that never blisters,
　　To the rain that never chills –
To the land of the waiting springtime,
　　To our five-meal, meat-fed men,
To the tall, deep-bosomed women,
　　And the children nine and ten!

And the children nine and ten (Stand up!),
    And the life we live and know,
Let a fellow sing o' the little things he cares about,
If a fellow fights for the little things he cares about
    With the weight of a twofold blow!

To the far-flung, fenceless prairie
    Where the quick cloud-shadows trail,
To our neighbour's barn in the offing
    And the line of the new-cut rail;
To the plough in her league-long furrow
    With the grey Lake gulls behind –
To the weight of a half-year's winter
    And the warm wet western wind!

To the home of the floods and thunder,
    To her pale dry healing blue –
To the lift of the great Cape combers,
    And the smell of the baked Karroo.
To the growl of the sluicing stamp-head –
    To the reef and the water-gold,
To the last and the largest Empire,
    To the map that is half unrolled!

To our dear dark foster-mothers,
    To the heathen songs they sung –
To the heathen speech we babbled
    Ere we came to the white man's tongue.
To the cool of our deep verandahs –
    To the blaze of our jewelled main,
To the night, to the palms in the moonlight,
    And the firefly in the cane!

To the hearth of Our People's People —
    To her well-ploughed windy sea,
To the hush of our dread high-altar
    Where The Abbey makes us We.
To the grist of the slow-ground ages,
    To the gain that is yours and mine —
To the Bank of the Open Credit,
    To the Powerhouse of the Line!

We've drunk to the Queen — God bless her!
    We've drunk to our mothers' land;
We've drunk to our English brother
    (And we hope he'll understand).
We've drunk as much as we're able,
    And the Cross swings low for the morn;
Last toast — and your foot on the table! —
    A health to the Native-born!

A health to the Native-born (Stand up!),
    We're six white men arow,
All bound to sing o' the little things we care about,
All bound to fight for the little things we care about
    With the weight of a sixfold blow!
By the might of our Cable-tow (Take hands!),
    From the Orkneys to the Horn
All round the world (and a little loop to pull it by),
All round the world (and a little strap to buckle it).
    A health to the Native-born!

MY BOY JACK

1914–18

'HAVE you news of my boy Jack?'
    Not this tide.
'When d'you think that he'll come back?'
    Not with this wind blowing, and this tide.

'Has anyone else had word of him?'
    Not this tide.
For what is sunk will hardly swim,
    Not with this wind blowing, and this tide.

'Oh, dear, what comfort can I find?'
    None this tide,
    Nor any tide,
Except he did not shame his kind —
    Not even with that wind blowing, and that tide.

Then hold your head up all the more,
    This tide,
    And every tide;
Because he was the son you bore,
    And gave to that wind blowing and that tide!

William Orpen, 'Ready to Start' (1917)

THE VAMPIRE

A FOOL there was and he made his prayer
(Even as you and I!)
To a rag and a bone and a hank of hair
(We called her the woman who did not care)
But the fool he called her his lady fair –
(Even as you and I!)

Oh, the years we waste and the tears we waste
And the work of our head and hand
Belong to the woman who did not know
(And now we know that she never could know)
And did not understand!

A fool there was and his goods he spent
(Even as you and I!)
Honour and faith and a sure intent
(And it wasn't the least what the lady meant)
But a fool must follow his natural bent
(Even as you and I!)

Oh, the toil we lost and the spoil we lost
And the excellent things we planned
Belong to the woman who didn't know why
(And now we know that she never knew why)
And did not understand!

The fool was stripped to his foolish hide
(Even as you and I!)
Which she might have seen when she threw him aside –
(But it isn't on record the lady tried)
So some of him lived but the most of him died –
(Even as you and I!)

And it isn't the shame and it isn't the blame
That stings like a white-hot brand –
It's coming to know that she never knew why
(Seeing, at last, she could never know why)
And never could understand!

THE ENGLISH FLAG

Above the portico a flagstaff, bearing the Union Jack,
remained fluttering in the flames for some time, but
ultimately when it fell the crowds rent the air with
shouts, and seemed to see significance in the incident.

Daily Papers

WINDS of the World, give answer!
        They are whimpering to and fro –
And what should they know of England
        who only England know? –
The poor little street-bred people
        that vapour and fume and brag,
They are lifting their heads in the stillness
        to yelp at the English Flag!

Must we borrow a clout from the Boer –
        to plaster anew with dirt?
An Irish liar's bandage, or an English coward's shirt?
We may not speak of England; her Flag's to sell or share.
'What is the Flag of England?
        Winds of the World, declare!

The North Wind blew: – 'From Bergen
        my steel-shod vanguards go;
I chase your lazy whalers home from the Disko floe.
By the great North Lights above me
        I work the will of God,
And the liner splits on the ice-field
        or the Dogger fills with cod.

'I barred my gates with iron,
                        I shuttered my doors with flame,
Because to force my ramparts your nutshell navies came.
I took the sun from their presence,
                        I cut them down with my blast,
And they died, but the Flag of England
                        blew free ere the spirit passed.

'The lean white bear hath seen it
                        in the long, long Arctic nights,
The musk-ox knows the standard
                        that flouts the Northern Lights:
What is the Flag of England?
                        Ye have but my bergs to dare,
Ye have but my drifts to conquer.
                        Go forth, for it is there!'

The South Wind sighed: – 'From the Virgins my
                        mid-sea course was ta'en
Over a thousand islands lost in an idle main,
Where the sea-egg flames on the coral
                        and the long-backed breakers croon
Their endless ocean legends to the lazy, locked lagoon.

'Strayed amid lonely islets, mazed amid outer keys,
I waked the palms to laughter –
                        I tossed the scud in the breeze.
Never was isle so little, never was sea so lone,
But over the scud and the palm-trees
                        an English flag was flown.

'I have wrenched it free from the halliards

                to hang for a wisp on the Horn;
I have chased it north to the Lizard –

                ribboned and rolled and torn;
I have spread its folds o'er the dying,

                adrift in a hopeless sea;
I have hurled it swift on the slaver,

                and seen the slave set free.

'My basking sunfish know it, and wheeling albatross,
Where the lone wave fills with fire

                beneath the Southern Cross.
What is the Flag of England?

                Ye have but my reefs to dare,
Ye have but my seas to furrow. Go forth, for it is there!'

The East Wind roared: – 'From the Kuriles,

                the Bitter Seas, I come,
And me men call the Home-Wind,

                for I bring the English home.
Look – look well to your shipping!

                By the breath of my mad typhoon
I swept your close-packed Praya

                and beached your best at Kowloon!

'The reeling junks behind me and the racing seas before,
I raped your richest roadstead – I plundered Singapore!
I set my hand on the Hoogli; as a hooded snake she rose;
And I flung your stoutest steamers
       to roost with the startled crows.

'Never the lotos closes, never the wildfowl wake,
But a soul goes out on the East Wind
        that died for England's sake –
Man or woman or suckling, mother or bride or maid –
Because on the bones of the English
       the English Flag is stayed.

'The desert-dust hath dimmed it,
       the flying wild-ass knows,
The scared white leopard winds it
       across the taintless snows.
What is the Flag of England? Ye have but my sun to dare,
Ye have but my sands to travel. Go forth, for it is there!'

The West Wind called: – 'In squadrons
       the thoughtless galleons fly
That bear the wheat and cattle
       lest street-bred people die.
They make my might their porter,
       they make my house their path,
Till I loose my neck from their rudder
       and whelm them all in my wrath.

'I draw the gliding fog-bank as a snake is drawn
                                        from the hole.
They bellow one to the other, the frighted ship-bells toll;
For day is a drifting terror till I raise the shroud
                                        with my breath,
And they see strange bows above them
                        and the two go locked to death.

'But whether in calm or wrack-wreath,
                        whether by dark or day,
I heave them whole to the conger
                        or rip their plates away,
First of the scattered legions, under a shrieking sky,
Dipping between the rollers, the English Flag goes by.

'The dead dumb fog hath wrapped it –
                the frozen dews have kissed –
The naked stars have seen it, a fellow-star in the mist.
What is the Flag of England?
                Ye have but my breath to dare,
Ye have but my waves to conquer.
                        Go forth, for it is there!'

WHEN EARTH'S LAST PICTURE IS PAINTED

L'Envoi to 'The Seven Seas'

WHEN earth's last picture is painted
    and the tubes are twisted and dried,
When the oldest colours have faded,
    and the youngest critic has died,
We shall rest, and, faith, we shall need it –
    lie down for an aeon or two,
Till the Master of All Good Workmen
    shall put us to work anew.

And those that were good shall be happy:
    they shall sit in a golden chair;
They shall splash at a ten-league canvas
    with brushes of comets' hair.
They shall find real saints to draw from –
    Magdalene, Peter, and Paul;
They shall work for an age at a sitting
    and never be tired at all!

And only The Master shall praise us,
    and only The Master shall blame;
And no one shall work for money,
    and no one shall work for fame,
But each for the joy of the working,
    and each, in his separate star,
Shall draw the Thing as he sees It
    for the God of Things as They are!

ULSTER

Their webs shall not become garments, neither shall they
cover themselves with their works: their works are works
of iniquity, and the act of violence is in their hands.

Isaiah 49:6

THE dark eleventh hour
Draws on and sees us sold
To every evil power
We fought against of old.
Rebellion, rapine, hate,
Oppression, wrong and greed
Are loosed to rule our fate,
By England's act and deed.

The Faith in which we stand,
The laws we made and guard –
Our honour, lives, and land –
Are given for reward
To Murder done by night,
To Treason taught by day,
To folly, sloth, and spite,
And we are thrust away.

The blood our fathers spilt,
Our love, our toils, our pains,
Are counted us for guilt,
And only bind our chains.
Before an Empire's eyes
The traitor claims his price.
What need of further lies?
We are the sacrifice.

We asked no more than leave
To reap where we had sown,
Through good and ill to cleave
To our own flag and throne.
Now England's shot and steel
Beneath that flag must show
How loyal hearts should kneel
To England's oldest foe.

We know the wars prepared
On every peaceful home,
We know the hells declared
For such as serve not Rome —
The terror, threats, and dread
In market, hearth, and field —
We know, when all is said,
We perish if we yield.

Believe, we dare not boast,
Believe, we do not fear —
We stand to pay the cost
In all that men hold dear.
What answer from the North?
One Law, one Land, one Throne.
If England drive us forth
We shall not fall alone!

The Ballad of East and West

*O*H, *East is East, and West is West,*
                           and never the twain shall meet,
Till Earth and Sky stand presently

                           at God's great Judgment Seat;
But there is neither East nor West, Border, nor Breed, nor Birth,
When two strong men stand face to face,
                           though they come from the ends of the earth!

Kamal is out with twenty men to raise the Border-side,
And he has lifted the Colonel's mare

                           that is the Colonel's pride.
He has lifted her out of the stable-door

                           between the dawn and the day,
And turned the calkins upon her feet,

                           and ridden her far away.
Then up and spoke the Colonel's son

                           that led a troop of the Guides:
'Is there never a man of all my men

                           can say where Kamal hides?'
Then up and spoke Mohammed Khan,

                           the son of the Ressaldar:
'If ye know the track of the morning-mist,

                           ye know where his pickets are.
At dusk he harries the Abazai —at dawn he is into Bonair,
But he must go by Fort Bukloh to his own place to fare.
So if ye gallop to Fort Bukloh as fast as a bird can fly,
By the favour of God ye may cut him off

                           ere he win to the Tongue of Jagai.

But if he be past the Tongue of Jagai,
                    right swiftly turn ye then,
For the length and the breadth of that grisly plain
                    is sown with Kamal's men.
There is rock to the left, and rock to the right,
                    and low lean thorn between,
And ye may hear a breech-bolt snick
                    where never a man is seen.'
The Colonel's son has taken horse,
                    and a raw rough dun was he,
With the mouth of a bell and the heart of Hell
                    and the head of a gallows-tree.
The Colonel's son to the Fort has won,
                    they bid him stay to eat –
Who rides at the tail of a Border thief,
                    he sits not long at his meat.
He's up and away from Fort Bukloh as fast as he can fly,
Till he was aware of his father's mare
                    in the gut of the Tongue of Jagai,
Till he was aware of his father's mare
                    with Kamal upon her back,
And when he could spy the white of her eye,
                    he made the pistol crack.
He has fired once, he has fired twice,
                    but the whistling ball went wide.
'Ye shoot like a soldier,' Kamal said.
                    'Show now if ye can ride!'
It's up and over the Tongue of Jagai,
                    as blown dust-devils go.
The dun he fled like a stag of ten,
                    but the mare like a barren doe.

The dun he leaned against the bit
                              and slugged his head above,
But the red mare played with the snaffle-bars,
                              as a maiden plays with a glove.
There was rock to the left and rock to the right,
                              and low lean thorn between,
And thrice he heard a breech-bolt snick
                              tho' never a man was seen.
They have ridden the low moon out of the sky,
                              their hoofs drum up the dawn,
The dun he went like a wounded bull,
                              but the mare like a new-roused fawn.
The dun he fell at a watercourse —
                              in a woeful heap fell he,
And Kamal has turned the red mare back,
                              and pulled the rider free.
He has knocked the pistol out of his hand —
                              small room was there to strive,
''Twas only by favour of mine,' quoth he,
                              'ye rode so long alive:
There was not a rock for twenty mile,
                              there was not a clump of tree,
But covered a man of my own men
                              with his rifle cocked on his knee.
If I had raised my bridle-hand, as I have held it low,
The little jackals that flee so fast
                              were feasting all in a row.
If I had bowed my head on my breast,
                              as I have held it high,
The kite that whistles above us now
                              were gorged till she could nat fly.'

Lightly answered the Colonel's son:
                'Do good to bird and beast,
But count who come for the broken meats
                before thou makest a feast.
If there should follow a thousand swords
                to carry my bones away,
Belike the price of a jackal's meal
                were more than a thief could pay.
They will feed their horse on the standing crop,
                their men on the garnered grain.
The thatch of the byres will serve their fires
                when all the cattle are slain.
But if thou thinkest the price be fair, –
                thy brethren wait to sup,
The hound is kin to the jackal-spawn, –
                howl, dog, and call them up!
And if thou thinkest the price be high,
                in steer and gear and stack,
Give me my father's mare again,
                and I'll fight my own way back!'
Kamal has gripped him by the hand
                and set him upon his feet.
'No talk shall be of dogs,' said he,
                'when wolf and grey wolf meet.
May I eat dirt if thou hast hurt of me in deed or breath;
What dam of lances brought thee forth
                to jest at the dawn with Death?'
Lightly answered the Colonel's son:
                'I hold by the blood of my clan:
Take up the mare for my father's gift –
                by God, she has carried a man!'

The red mare ran to the Colonel's son,
                and nuzzled against his breast;
'We be two strong men,' said Kamal then,
                'but she loveth the younger best.
So she shall go with a lifter's dower,
                my turquoise-studded rein,
My 'broidered saddle and saddle-cloth,
                and silver stirrups twain.'
The Colonel's son a pistol drew, and held it muzzle-end,
'Ye have taken the one from a foe,' said he.
                'Will ye take the mate from a friend?'
'A gift for a gift,' said Kamal straight;
                'a limb for the risk of a limb.
'Thy father has sent his son to me,
                I'll send my son to him!'
With that he whistled his only son,
                that dropped from a mountain crest –
He trod the ling like a buck in spring,
                and he looked like a lance in rest.
'Now here is thy master,' Kamal said,
                'who leads a troop of the Guides,
And thou must ride at his left side
                as shield on shoulder rides.
Till Death or I cut loose the tie,
                at camp and board and bed,
Thy life is his – thy fate it is to guard him with thy head.
So, thou must eat the White Queen's meat,
                and all her foes are thine,
And thou must harry thy father's hold
                for the peace of the Borderline.

And thou must make a trooper tough
                        and hack thy way to power –
Belike they will raise thee to Ressaldar
                        when I am hanged in Peshawur!'

They have looked each other between the eyes,
                        and there they found no fault.
They have taken the Oath of the Brother-in-Blood
                        on leavened bread and salt:
They have taken the Oath of the Brother-in-Blood
                        on fire and fresh-cut sod,
On the hilt and the haft of the Khyber knife,
                        and the Wondrous Names of God.
The Colonel's son he rides the mare
                        and Kamal's boy the dun,
And two have come back to Fort Bukloh
                        where there went forth but one.
And when they drew to the Quarter-Guard,
                        full twenty swords flew clear –
There was not a man but carried his feud
                        with the blood of the mountaineer.
'Ha' done! ha' done!' said the Colonel's son.
                        'Put up the steel at your sides!
Last night ye had struck at a Border thief –
                        tonight 'tis a man of the Guides!'

Oh, East is East, and West is West,
                        and never the twain shall meet,
Till Earth and Sky stand presently
                        at God's great Judgment Seat;
But there is neither East nor West, Border, nor Breed, nor Birth,
When two strong men stand face to face,
                        though they come from the ends of the earth!

A DEATH-BED

'THIS is the State above the Law.
    The State exists for the State alone.'
[*This is a gland at the back of the jaw,*
And an answering lump by the collar-bone.]

Some die shouting in gas or fire;
Some die silent, by shell and shot.
Some die desperate, caught on the wire;
Some die suddenly. This will not.

'Regis suprema voluntas Lex'
[*It will follow the regular course of – throats.*]
Some die pinned by the broken-decks,
Some die sobbing between the boats.

Some die eloquent, pressed to death
By the sliding trench, as their friends can hear.
Some die wholly in half a breath.
Some – give trouble for half a year.

'There is neither Evil nor Good in life
Except as the needs of the State ordain.'
[*Since it is rather too late for the knife,*
All we can do is to mask the pain.]

Some die saintly in faith and hope —
One died thus in a prison-yard —
Some die broken by rape or the rope;
Some die easily. This dies hard.

'I will dash to pieces who bar my way.
Woe to the traitor! Woe to the weak!'
[*Let him write what he wishes to say.*
It tires him out if he tries to speak.]

Some die quietly. Some abound
In loud self-pity. Others spread
Bad morale through the cots around ...
This is a type that is better dead.

'The war was forced on me by my foes.
All that I sought was the right to live.'
[*Don't be afraid of a triple dose;*
The pain will neutralise half we give.

Here are the needles. See that he dies
While the effects of the drug endure ...
What is the question he asks with his eyes? —
Yes, All-Highest, to God, be sure.]

THE VIRGINITY

TRY as he will, no man breaks wholly loose
   From his first love, no matter who she be.
Oh, was there ever sailor free to choose,
   That didn't settle somewhere near the sea?

Myself, it don't excite me nor amuse
   To watch a pack o' shipping on the sea;
But I can understand my neighbour's views
   From certain things which have occurred to me.

Men must keep touch with things they used to use
   To earn their living, even when they are free;
And so come back upon the least excuse –
   Same as the sailor settled near the sea.

He knows he's never going on no cruise –
   He knows he's done and finished with the sea;
And yet he likes to feel she's there to use –
   If he should ask her – as she used to be.

Even though she cost him all he had to lose,
   Even though she made him sick to hear or see,
Still, what she left of him will mostly choose
   Her skirts to sit by. How comes such to be?

Parsons in pulpits, taxpayers in pews,
   Kings on your thrones, you know as well as me,
We've only one virginity to lose,
   And where we lost it there our hearts will be!

THE WAGE-SLAVES

OH, Glorious are the guarded heights
    Where guardian souls abide –
Self-exiled from our gross delights –
    Above, beyond, outside:
An ampler arc their spirit swings –
    Commands a juster view –
We have their word for all these things,
    No doubt their words are true.

Yet we, the bondslaves of our day,
    Whom dirt and danger press –
Co-heirs of insolence, delay,
    And leagued unfaithfulness –
Such is our need must seek indeed
    And, having found, engage
The men who merely do the work
    For which they draw the wage.

From forge and farm and mine and bench,
    Deck, altar, outpost lone –
Mill, school, battalion, counter, trench,
    Rail, senate, sheepfold, throne –
Creation's cry goes up on high
    From age to cheated age:
'Send us the men who do the work
    For which they draw the wage!'

Words cannot help nor wit achieve,
    Nor e'en the all-gifted fool,
Too weak to enter, bide, or leave
    The lists he cannot rule.
Beneath the sun we count on none
    Our evil to assuage,
Except the men that do the work
    For which they draw the wage.

When through the Gates of Stress and Strain
    Comes forth the vast Event —
The simple, sheer, sufficing, sane
    Result of labour spent —
They that have wrought the end unthought
    Be neither saint nor sage,
But only men who did the work
    For which they drew the wage.

Wherefore to these the Fates shall bend
    (And all old idle things)
Wherefore on these shall Power attend
    Beyond the grip of kings:
Each in his place, by right, not grace,
    Shall rule his heritage —
The men who simply do the work
    For which they draw the wage.

Not such as scorn the loitering street,
    Or waste, to earn its praise,
Their noontide's unreturning heat
    About their morning ways;
But such as dower each mortgaged hour
    Alike with clean courage –
Even the men who do the work
    For which they draw the wage –
Men, like to Gods, that do the work
    For which they draw the wage –
Begin – continue – close that work
    For which they draw the wage!

TOMLINSON

Now Tomlinson gave up the ghost
        at his house in Berkeley Square,
And a Spirit came to his bedside
        and gripped him by the hair –
A Spirit gripped him by the hair
        and carried him far away,
Till he heard as the roar of a rain-fed ford
        the roar of the Milky Way:
Till he heard the roar of the Milky Way
        die down and drone and cease,
And they came to the Gate within the Wall
        where Peter holds the keys.
'Stand up, stand up now, Tomlinson,
        and answer loud and high
The good that ye did for the sake of men
        or ever ye came to die –
The good that ye did for the sake of men
        on little Earth so lone!'
And the naked soul of Tomlinson
        grew white as a rain-washed bone.
'O I have a friend on Earth,' he said,
        'that was my priest and guide,
And well would he answer all for me
        if he were at my side.'
– 'For that ye strove in neighbour-love
        it shall be written fair,
But now ye wait at Heaven's Gate
        and not in Berkeley Square:

Though we called your friend from his bed this night,
                          he could not speak for you,
For the race is run by one and one
                          and never by two and two.'
Then Tomlinson looked up and down,
                          and little gain was there,
For the naked stars grinned overhead,
                          and he saw that his soul was bare.
The Wind that blows between the Worlds,
                          it cut him like a knife,
And Tomlinson took up the tale
                          and spoke of his good in life.
'O this I have read in a book,' he said,
                          'and that was told to me,
And this I have thought that another man thought
                          of a Prince in Muscovy.'
The good souls flocked like homing doves
                          and bade him clear the path,
And Peter twirled the jangling Keys
                          in weariness and wrath.
'Ye have read, ye have heard, ye have thought,' he said,
                          'and the tale is yet to run:
By the worth of the body that once ye had,
                          give answer – what ha' ye done?'
Then Tomlinson looked back and forth,
                          and little good it bore,
For the darkness stayed at his shoulder-blade
                          and Heaven's Gate before: –
'O this I have felt, and this I have guessed,
                          and this I have heard men say,
And this they wrote that another man wrote
                          of a carl in Norroway.'

'Ye have read, ye have felt, ye have guessed, good lack!
                    Ye have hampered Heaven's Gate;
There's little room between the stars
                              in idleness to prate!
For none may reach by hired speech
                        of neighbour, priest, and kin
Through borrowed deed to God's good meed
                              that lies so fair within;
Get hence, get hence to the Lord of Wrong,
                        for the doom has yet to run,
And ... the faith that ye share with Berkeley Square
                        uphold you, Tomlinson!'

* * *

The Spirit gripped him by the hair,
                        and sun by sun they fell
Till they came to the belt of Naughty Stars
                              that rim the mouth of Hell.
The first are red with pride and wrath,
                        the next are white with pain,
But the third are black with clinkered sin
                              that cannot burn again.
They may hold their path, they may leave their path,
                        with never a soul to mark:
They may burn or freeze, but they must not cease
                        in the Scorn of the Outer Dark.
The Wind that blows between the Worlds,
                        it nipped him to the bone,
And he yearned to the flare of Hell-gate there
                        as the light of his own hearthstone.

The Devil he sat behind the bars,
               where the desperate legions drew,
But he caught the hasting Tomlinson
               and would not let him through.
'Wot ye the price of good pit-coal
               that I must pay?' said he,
'That ye rank yoursel' so fit for Hell
               and ask no leave of me?
I am all o'er-sib to Adam's breed
               that ye should give me scorn,
For I strove with God for your First Father
               the day that he was born.
Sit down, sit down upon the slag,
               and answer loud and high
The harm that ye did to the Sons of Men
               or ever you came to die.'
And Tomlinson looked up and up,
               and saw against the night
The belly of a tortured star
               blood-red in Hell-Mouth light;
And Tomlinson looked down and down,
               and saw beneath his feet
The frontlet of a tortured star
               milk-white in Hell-Mouth heat.
'O I had a love on earth,' said he,
               'that kissed me to my fall;
And if ye would call my love to me
               I know she would answer all.'
– 'All that ye did in love forbid it shall be written fair,
But now ye wait at Hell-Mouth Gate
               and not in Berkeley Square:

Though we whistled your love from her bed tonight,
>> I trow she would not run,
For the sin ye do by two and two
>> ye must pay for one by one!'
The Wind that blows between the Worlds,
>> it cut him like a knife,
And Tomlinson took up the tale
>> and spoke of his sins in life: —
'Once I ha' laughed at the power of Love
>> and twice at the grip of the Grave,
And thrice I ha' patted my God on the head
>> that men might call me brave.'
The Devil he blew on a brandered soul
>> and set it aside to cool: —
'Do ye think I would waste my good pit-coal
>> on the hide of a brain-sick fool?
I see no worth in the hobnailed mirth
>> or the jolthead jest ye did
That I should waken my gentlemen
>> that are sleeping three on a grid.'
Then Tomlinson looked back and forth,
>> and there was little grace,
For Hell-Gate filled the houseless soul
>> with the Fear of Naked Space.
'Nay, this I ha' heard,' quo' Tomlinson,
>> 'and this was noised abroad,
And this I ha' got from a Belgian book
>> on the word of a dead French lord.'
— 'Ye ha' heard, ye ha' read, ye ha' got, good lack!
>> and the tale begins afresh —
Have ye sinned one sin for the pride o' the eye
>> or the sinful lust of the flesh?'

Then Tomlinson he gripped the bars
              and yammered, 'Let me in –
For I mind that I borrowed my neighbour's wife
              to sin the deadly sin.
The Devil he grinned behind the bars,
              and banked the fires high:
'Did ye read of that sin in a book?' said he;
              and Tomlinson said, 'Ay!'
The Devil he blew upon his nails, and the little devils ran,
And he said: 'Go husk this whimpering thief
              that comes in the guise of a man:
Winnow him out 'twixt star and star,
              and sieve his proper worth:
There's sore decline in Adam's line
              if this be spawn of Earth.'
Empusa's crew, so naked-new they may not face the fire,
But weep that they bin too small to sin
              to the height of their desire,
Over the coal they chased the Soul,
              and racked it all abroad,
As children rifle a caddis-case
              or the raven's foolish hoard.
And back they came with the tattered Thing,
              as children after play,
And they said: 'The soul that he got from God
              he has bartered clean away.
We have threshed a stook of print and book,
              and winnowed a chattering wind,
And many a soul wherefrom he stole,
              but his we cannot find.

We have handled him, we have dandled him,
                    we have seared him to the bone,
And, Sire, if tooth and nail show truth
                    he has no soul of his own.'
The Devil he bowed his head on his breast
                    and rumbled deep and low: —
'I'm all o'er-sib to Adam's breed
                    that I should bid him go.
Yet close we lie, and deep we lie, and if I gave him place,
My gentlemen that are so proud
                    would flout me to my face;
They'd call my house a common stews
                    and me a careless host,
And — I would not anger my gentlemen
                    for the sake of a shiftless ghost.'
The Devil he looked at the mangled Soul
                    that prayed to feel the flame,
And he thought of Holy Charity,
                    but he thought of his own good name: —
'Now ye could haste my coal to waste,
                    and sit ye down to fry.
Did ye think of that theft for yourself?' said he;
                    and Tomlinson said, 'Ay!'
The Devil he blew an outward breath,
                    for his heart was free from care: —
'Ye have scarce the soul of a louse,' he said,
                    'but the roots of sin are there,
And for that sin should ye come in were I the lord alone,
But sinful pride has rule inside —
                    ay, mightier than my own.

Honour and Wit, fore-damned they sit,
                    to each his Priest and Whore;
Nay, scarce I dare myself go there,
                    and you they'd torture sore.
Ye are neither spirit nor spirk,' he said;
                    'ye are neither book nor brute –
Go, get ye back to the flesh again
                    for the sake of Man's repute.
I'm all o'er-sib to Adam's breed
                    that I should mock your pain,
But look that ye win to worthier sin
                    ere ye come back again.
Get hence, the hearse is at your door –
                    the grim black stallions wait –
They bear your clay to place today.
                    Speed, lest ye come too late!
Go back to Earth with a lip unsealed –
                    go back with an open eye,
And carry my word to the Sons of Men
                    or ever ye come to die:
That the sin they do by two and two
                    they must pay for one by one,
And … the God that you took from a printed book
                    be with you, Tomlinson!'

THE WHITE MAN'S BURDEN

The United States and the Philippine Islands

TAKE up the White Man's burden –
  Send forth the best ye breed –
Go bind your sons to exile
  To serve your captives' need;
To wait in heavy harness
  On fluttered folk and wild –
Your new-caught, sullen peoples,
  Half devil and half child.

Take up the White Man's Burden –
  In patience to abide,
To veil the threat of terror
  And check the show of pride;
By open speech and simple,
  An hundred times made plain,
To seek another's profit,
  And work another's gain.

Take up the White Man's burden —
   The savage wars of peace —
Fill full the mouth of Famine
   And bid the sickness cease;
And when your goal is nearest
   The end for others sought,
Watch Sloth and heathen Folly
   Bring all your hope to nought.

Take up the White Man's burden —
   No tawdry rule of kings,
But toil of serf and sweeper —
   The tale of common things.
The ports ye shall not enter,
   The roads ye shall not tread,
Go make them with your living,
   And mark them with your dead!

Take up the White Man's burden
   And reap his old reward:
The blame of those ye better,
   The hate of those ye guard —
The cry of hosts ye humour
   (Ah, slowly!) toward the light: —
'Why brought ye us from bondage,
   Our loved Egyptian night?'

Take up the White Man's burden —
    Ye dare not stoop to less —
Nor call too loud on Freedom
    To cloak your weariness;
By all ye cry or whisper,
    By all ye leave or do,
The silent, sullen peoples
    Shall weigh your Gods and you.

Take up the White Man's burden —
    Have done with childish days —
The lightly proffered laurel,
    The easy, ungrudged praise.
Comes now, to search your manhood
    Through all the thankless years,
Cold-edged with dear-bought wisdom,
    The judgment of your peers!

'WHEN 'OMER SMOTE 'IS BLOOMIN' LYRE'

Introduction to the Barrack-Room Ballads in The Seven Seas

WHEN 'Omer smote 'is bloomin' lyre,
  He'd 'eard men sing by land an' sea;
An' what he thought 'e might require,
  'E went an' took – the same as me!

The market-girls an' fishermen,
  The shepherds an' the sailors, too,
They 'eard old songs turn up again,
  But kep' it quiet – same as you!

They knew 'e stole; 'e knew they knowed.
  They didn't tell, nor make a fuss,
But winked at 'Omer down the road,
An' 'e winked back – the same as us!

GUNGA DIN

You may talk o' gin and beer
  When you're quartered safe out 'ere,
An' you're sent to penny-fights an' Aldershot it;
But when it comes to slaughter
You will do your work on water,
An' you'll lick the bloomin' boots of 'im that's got it.
Now in Injia's sunny clime,
Where I used to spend my time
A-servin' of 'Er Majesty the Queen,
Of all them blackfaced crew
The finest man I knew
Was our regimental bhisti, Gunga Din.
    He was 'Din! Din! Din!
  You limpin' lump o' brick-dust, Gunga Din!
    Hi! Slippy *hitherao*!
    Water, get it! *Panee lao*,
  You squidgy-nosed old idol, Gunga Din.'

The uniform 'e wore
Was nothin' much before,
An' rather less than 'arf o' that be'ind,
For a piece o' twisty rag
An' a goatskin water-bag
Was all the field-equipment 'e could find.
When the sweatin' troop-train lay
In a sidin' through the day,
Where the 'eat would make
                your bloomin' eyebrows crawl,
We shouted 'Harry By!'
Till our throats were bricky-dry,
Then we wopped 'im 'cause 'e couldn't serve us all.
    It was 'Din! Din! Din!

You 'eathen, where the mischief 'ave you been?
 You put some *juldee* in it
 Or I'll *marrow* you this minute
If you don't fill up my helmet, Gunga Din!'

'E would dot an' carry one
Till the longest day was done;
An' 'e didn't seem to know the use o' fear.
If we charged or broke or cut,
You could bet your bloomin' nut,
'E'd be waitin' fifty paces right flank rear.
With 'is mussick on 'is back,
'E would skip with our attack,
An' watch us till the bugles made 'Retire,'
An' for all 'is dirty 'ide
'E was white, clear white, inside
When 'e went to tend the wounded under fire!
 It was 'Din! Din! Din!'
 With the bullets kickin' dust-spots on the green
  When the cartridges ran out,
  You could hear the front-ranks shout,
 'Hi! ammunition-mules an' Gunga Din!'

I shan't forgit the night
When I dropped be'ind the fight
With a bullet where my belt-plate should 'a' been.
I was chokin' mad with thirst,
An' the man that spied me first
Was our good old grinnin', gruntin' Gunga Din.

'E lifted up my 'ead,
An' he plugged me where I bled,
An' 'e guv me 'arf-a-pint o' water green.
It was crawlin' and it stunk,
But of all the drinks I've drunk,
I'm gratefullest to one from Gunga Din.
      It was 'Din! Din! Din!
    'Ere's a beggar with a bullet through 'is spleen;
     'E's chawin' up the ground,
      An' 'e's kickin' all around:
    For Gawd's sake git the water, Gunga Din!'

'E carried me away
To where a dooli lay,
An' a bullet come an' drilled the beggar clean.
'E put me safe inside,
An' just before 'e died,
'I 'ope you liked your drink,' sez Gunga Din.
So I'll meet 'im later on
At the place where 'e is gone –
Where it's always double drill and no canteen.
'E'll be squattin' on the coals
Givin' drink to poor damned souls,
An' I'll get a swig in hell from Gunga Din!
      Yes, Din! Din! Din!
    You Lazarushian-leather Gunga Din!
     Though I've belted you and flayed you,
     By the livin' Gawd that made you,
    You're a better man than I am, Gunga Din!

MANDALAY

By the old Moulmein Pagoda, lookin' lazy at the sea,
There's a Burma girl a-settin',
     and I know she thinks o' me;
For the wind is in the palm-trees,
     and the temple-bells they say:
'Come you back, you British soldier;
     come you back to Mandalay!'
  Come you back to Mandalay,
  Where the old Flotilla lay:
  Can't you 'ear their paddles chunkin'
     from Rangoon to Mandalay?
  On the road to Mandalay,
  Where the flyin'-fishes play,
  An' the dawn comes up like thunder
     outer China 'crost the Bay!

'Er petticoat was yaller an' 'er little cap was green,
An' 'er name was Supi-yaw-lat –
     jes' the same as Theebaw's Queen,
An' I seed her first a-smokin'
     of a whackin' white cheroot,
An' a-wastin' Christian kisses on an 'eathen idol's foot:
  Bloomin' idol made o' mud –
  Wot they called the Great Gawd Budd –
  Plucky lot she cared for idols
     when I kissed 'er where she stud!
  On the road to Mandalay ...

When the mist was on the rice-fields
                 an' the sun was droppin' slow,
She'd git 'er little banjo an' she'd sing '*Kulla-lo-lo!*'
With 'er arm upon my shoulder
                 an' 'er cheek agin my cheek
We useter watch the steamers an' the *hathis* pilin' teak.
    Elephints a-pilin' teak
    In the sludgy, squdgy creek,
    Where the silence 'ung that 'eavy
                 you was 'arf afraid to speak!
    On the road to Mandalay ...

But that's all shove be'ind me – long ago an' fur away,
An' there ain't no 'buses runnin'
                 from the Bank to Mandalay;
An' I'm learnin' 'ere in London
                 what the ten-year soldier tells:
'If you've 'eard the East a-callin',
                 you won't never 'eed naught else.'
    No! you won't 'eed nothin' else
    But them spicy garlic smells,
    An' the sunshine an' the palm-trees
                 an' the tinkly temple-bells;
    On the road to Mandalay ...

I am sick o' wastin' leather on these gritty pavin'-stones,
An' the blasted English drizzle

      wakes the fever in my bones;
Tho' I walks with fifty 'ousemaids

      outer Chelsea to the Strand,
An' they talks a lot o' lovin',

      but wot do they understand?
    Beefy face an' grubby 'and –
    Law! wot do they understand?
    I've a neater, sweeter maiden

      in a cleaner, greener land!
    On the road to Mandalay ...

Ship me somewheres east of Suez,

      where the best is like the worst,
Where there aren't no Ten Commandments

      an' a man can raise a thirst;
For the temple-bells are callin',

      an' it's there that I would be –
By the old Moulmein Pagoda, looking lazy at the sea;
    On the road to Mandalay,
    Where the old Flotilla lay,
    With our sick beneath the awnings

      when we went to Mandalay!
    On the road to Mandalay,
    Where the flyin'-fishes play,
    An' the dawn comes up like thunder

      outer China 'crost the Bay!

THE FEMALE OF THE SPECIES

WHEN the Himalayan peasant
    meets the he-bear in his pride,
He shouts to scare the monster,
    who will often turn aside.
But the she-bear thus accosted
    rends the peasant tooth and nail.
For the female of the species
    is more deadly than the male.

When Nag the basking cobra
    hears the careless foot of man,
He will sometimes wriggle sideways
    and avoid it if he can.
But his mate makes no such motion
    where she camps beside the trail.
For the female of the species
    is more deadly than the male.

When the early Jesuit fathers
    preached to Hurons and Choctaws,
They prayed to be delivered
    from the vengeance of the squaws.
'Twas the women, not the warriors,
    turned those stark enthusiasts pale.
For the female of the species
    is more deadly than the male.

Man's timid heart is bursting
                          with the things he must not say,
For the Woman that God gave him isn't his to give away;
But when hunter meets with husband,
                          each confirms the other's tale –
The female of the species is more deadly than the male.

Man, a bear in most relations –
                          worm and savage otherwise, –
Man propounds negotiations,
                          Man accepts the compromise.
Very rarely will he squarely push the logic of a fact
To its ultimate conclusion in unmitigated act.

Fear, or foolishness, impels him,
                          ere he lay the wicked low,
To concede some form of trial even to his fiercest foe.
Mirth obscene diverts his anger –
                          Doubt and Pity oft perplex
Him in dealing with an issue – to the scandal of The Sex!

But the Woman that God gave him,
                          every fibre of her frame
Proves her launched for one sole issue,
                          armed and engined for the same;
And to serve that single issue, lest the generations fail,
The female of the species must be deadlier than the male.

She who faces Death by torture
>for each life beneath her breast
May not deal in doubt or pity –
>must not swerve for fact or jest.
These be purely male diversions –
>not in these her honour dwells.
She the Other Law we live by,
>is that Law and nothing else.

She can bring no more to living
>than the powers that make her great
As the Mother of the Infant and the Mistress of the Mate.
And when Babe and Man are lacking
>and she strides unclaimed to claim
Her right as femme (and baron),
>her equipment is the same.

She is wedded to convictions – in default of grosser ties;
Her contentions are her children,
>Heaven help him who denies! –
He will meet no suave discussion,
>but the instant, white-hot, wild,
Wakened female of the species
>warring as for spouse and child.

Unprovoked and awful charges –
                     even so the she-bear fights,
Speech that drips, corrodes, and poisons –
                     even so the cobra bites,
Scientific vivisection of one nerve till it is raw
And the victim writhes in anguish –
                     like the Jesuit with the squaw!

So it comes that Man, the coward,
                     when he gathers to confer
With his fellow-braves in council,
                     dare not leave a place for her
Where, at war with Life and Conscience,
                     he uplifts his erring hands
To some God of Abstract Justice –
                     which no woman understands.

And Man knows it! Knows, moreover,
                     that the Woman that God gave him
Must command but may not govern –
                     shall enthral but not enslave him.
And *She* knows, because She warns him,
                     and Her instincts never fail
That the Female of Her Species
                     is more deadly than the Male.

THAT DAY

IT got beyond all orders an' it got beyond all 'ope;
  It got to shammin' wounded an' retirin' from the 'alt.
'Ole companies was lookin' for the nearest road to slope;
   It were just a bloomin' knock-out – an' our fault!

> *Now there ain't no chorus 'ere to give,*
>   *Nor there ain't no band to play;*
> *An' I wish I was dead 'fore I done what I did,*
>   *Or seen what I seed that day!*

We was sick o' bein' punished,
                 an' we let 'em know it, too;
  An' a company-commander up an 'it us with a sword,
An' some one shouted ''Ook it!'
               an' it come to *sove-ki-poo*,
  An' we chucked our rifles from us – O my Gawd!

There was thirty dead an' wounded
             on the ground we wouldn't keep –
  No, there wasn't more than twenty
             when the front begun to go –
But, Christ! along the line o' flight
            they cut us up like sheep,
  An' that was all we gained by doin' so!

I 'eard the knives be'ind me, but I dursn't face my man,
  Nor I don't know where I went to,
              'cause I didn't 'alt to see,
Till I 'eard a beggar squealin' out for quarter as 'e ran,
  An' I thought I knew the voice an' – it was me!

We was 'idin' under bedsteads
                    more than 'arf a march away:
   We was lyin' up like rabbits all about the countryside;
An' the Major cursed 'is Maker
                    'cause 'e'd lived to see that day,
   An' the Colonel broke 'is sword acrost, an' cried.

We was rotten 'fore we started –
                    we was never *disciplined*;
   We made it out a favour if an order was obeyed.
Yes, every little drummer
                    'ad 'is rights an' wrongs to mind,
   So we had to pay for teachin' – an' we paid!

The papers 'id it 'andsome,
                    but you know the Army knows;
   We was put to groomin' camels
                    till the regiments withdrew.
An' they gave us each a medal
                    for subduin' England's foes,
   An' I 'ope you like my song – because it's true!

> *An' there ain't no chorus 'ere to give,*
>   *Nor there ain't no band to play;*
> *But I wish I was dead 'fore I done what I did,*
>   *Or seen what I seed that day!*

DANNY DEEVER

'WHAT are the bugles blowin' for?'
                    said Files-on-Parade.
'To turn you out, to turn you out,'
                    the Colour-Sergeant said.
'What makes you look so white, so white?'
                    said Files-on-Parade.
'I'm dreadin' what I've got to watch,'
                    the Colour-Sergeant said.
  For they're hangin' Danny Deever,
                    you can hear the Dead March play,
  The Regiment's in 'ollow square –
                    they're hangin' him today;
  They've taken of his buttons off
                    an' cut his stripes away,
  An' they're hangin' Danny Deever in the mornin'.

'What makes the rear-rank breathe so 'ard?'
                    said Files-on-Parade.
'It's bitter cold, it's bitter cold,'
                    the Colour-Sergeant said.
'What makes that front-rank man fall down?'
                    said Files-on-Parade.
'A touch o' sun, a touch o' sun,'
                    the Colour-Sergeant said.
  They are hangin' Danny Deever,
                    they are marchin' of 'im round,
  They 'ave 'alted Danny Deever
                    by 'is coffin on the ground;
  An' 'e'll swing in 'arf a minute
                    for a sneakin' shootin' hound –
  O they're hangin' Danny Deever in the mornin'!

''Is cot was right-'and cot to mine,' said Files-on-Parade.
''E's sleepin' out an' far tonight,'
                  the Colour-Sergeant said.
'I've drunk 'is beer a score o' times,'
                  said Files-on-Parade.
''E's drinkin' bitter beer alone,'
                  the Colour-Sergeant said.
  They are hangin' Danny Deever,
                  you must mark 'im to 'is place,
  For 'e shot a comrade sleepin' –
                  you must look 'im in the face;
  Nine 'undred of 'is county
                  an' the Regiment's disgrace,
  While they're hangin' Danny Deever in the mornin'.

'What's that so black agin the sun?' said Files-on-Parade.
'It's Danny fightin' 'ard for life,'
                  the Colour-Sergeant said.
'What's that that whimpers over'ead?'
                  said Files-on-Parade.
'It's Danny's soul that's passin' now,'
                  the Colour Sergeant said.
  For they're done with Danny Deever,
                  you can 'ear the quickstep play,
  The Regiment's in column,
                  an' they're marchin' us away;
  Ho! the young recruits are shakin',
                  an' they'll want their beer today,
  After hangin' Danny Deever in the mornin'!

CHANT-PAGAN

English Irregular, discharged

M E that 'ave been what I've been –
  Me that 'ave gone where I've gone –
Me that 'ave seen what I've seen –
  'Ow can I ever take on
With awful old England again,
  An' 'ouses both sides of the street,
And 'edges two sides of the lane,
  And the parson an' gentry between,
An' touchin' my 'at when we meet –
    Me that 'ave been what I've been?

Me that 'ave watched 'arf a world
  'Eave up all shiny with dew,
Kopje on kop to the sun,
  An' as soon as the mist let 'em through
Our 'elios winkin' like fun –
  Three sides of a ninety-mile square,
Over valleys as big as a shire –
  'Are ye there? Are ye there? Are ye there?'
An' then the blind drum of our fire ...
  An' I'm rollin' 'is lawns for the Squire,
      Me!

Me that 'ave rode through the dark
Forty mile, often, on end,
Along the Ma'ollisberg Range,
With only the stars for my mark
An' only the night for my friend,
An' things runnin' off as you pass,
An' things jumpin' up in the grass,
An' the silence, the shine an' the size
Of the 'igh, unexpressible skies –
I am takin' some letters almost
As much as a mile to the post,
An' 'mind you come back with the change!'
   Me!

Me that saw Barberton took
When we dropped through the clouds on their 'ead,
An' they 'ove the guns over and fled –
Me that was through Di'mond 'Ill,
An' Pieters an' Springs an' Belfast –
From Dundee to Vereeniging all –
Me that stuck out to the last
(An' five bloomin' bars on my chest) –
I am doin' my Sunday-school best,
By the 'elp of the Squire an' 'is wife
(Not to mention the 'ousemaid an' cook),
To come in an' 'ands up an' be still,
An' honestly work for my bread,
My livin' in that state of life
To which it shall please God to call
   Me!

Me that 'ave followed my trade
In the place where the Lightnin's are made;
'Twixt the Rains and the Sun and the Moon –
Me that lay down an' got up
Three years with the sky for my roof –
That 'ave ridden my 'unger an' thirst
Six thousand raw mile on the hoof,
With the Vaal and the Orange for cup,
An' the Brandwater Basin for dish, –
Oh! it's 'ard to be'ave as they wish
(Too 'ard, an' a little too soon),
I'll 'ave to think over it first –
      Me!

I will arise an' get 'ence –
I will trek South and make sure
If it's only my fancy or not
That the sunshine of England is pale,
And the breezes of England are stale,
An' there's somethin' gone small with the lot.
For I know of a sun an' a wind,
An' some plains and a mountain be'ind,
An' some graves by a barb-wire fence,
An' a Dutchman I've fought 'oo might give
Me a job were I ever inclined
To look in an' offsaddle an' live
Where there's neither a road nor a tree –
But only my Maker an' me,
And I think it will kill me or cure,
So I think I will go there an' see.
      Me!

TOMMY

I WENT into a public 'ouse to get a pint o' beer,
The publican 'e up an' sez,

'We serve no redcoats here.'
The girls be'ind the bar they laughed

an' giggled fit to die,
I outs into the street again an' to myself sez I:
  O it's Tommy this, an' Tommy that,

an' Tommy, go away';
  But it's 'Thank you, Mister Atkins,'

when the band begins to play –
  The band begins to play, my boys,

the band begins to play,
  O it's 'Thank you, Mister Atkins,'

when the band begins to play.

I went into a theatre as sober as could be,
They gave a drunk civilian room, but 'adn't none for me;
They sent me to the gallery or round the music-'alls,
But when it comes to fightin', Lord!

they'll shove me in the stalls!
  For it's Tommy this, an' Tommy that,

an' Tommy, wait outside';
  But it's 'Special train for Atkins'

when the trooper's on the tide –
  The troopship's on the tide, my boys,

the troopship's on the tide,
  O it's 'Special train for Atkins'

when the trooper's on the tide.

Yes, makin' mock o' uniforms
> that guard you while you sleep
Is cheaper than them uniforms,
> an' they're starvation cheap;
An' hustlin' drunken soldiers
> when they're goin' large a bit
Is five times better business than paradin' in full kit.
> Then it's Tommy this, an' Tommy that,
> > an' 'Tommy, 'ow's yer soul?'
> But it's 'Thin red line of 'eroes'
> > when the drums begin to roll —
> The drums begin to roll, my boys,
> > the drums begin to roll,
> O it's 'Thin red line of 'eroes'
> > when the drums begin to roll.

We aren't no thin red 'eroes,
> nor we aren't no blackguards too,
But single men in barracks, most remarkable like you;
An' if sometimes our conduck isn't all your fancy paints,
Why, single men in barracks
> don't grow into plaster saints;
> While it's Tommy this, an' Tommy that,
> > an' 'Tommy, fall be'ind,'
> But it's 'Please to walk in front, sir,'
> > when there's trouble in the wind —
> There's trouble in the wind, my boys,
> > there's trouble in the wind,
> O it's 'Please to walk in front, sir,'
> > when there's trouble in the wind.

You talk o' better food for us,

     an' schools, an' fires, an' all:
We'll wait for extry rations if you treat us rational.
Don't mess about the cook room slops,

      but prove it to our face
The Widow's Uniform is not the soldier-man's disgrace.
 For it's Tommy this, an' Tommy that,

     an' 'Chuck him out, the brute!'
 But it's 'Saviour of 'is country'

     when the guns begin to shoot;
 An' it's Tommy this, an' Tommy that,

     an' anything you please;
 An' Tommy ain't a bloomin' fool —

     you bet that Tommy sees!

'Fuzzy-Wuzzy'

Soudan Expeditionary Force. Early Campaigns

WE'VE fought with many men acrost the seas,
  An' some of 'em was brave an' some was not:
The Paythan an' the Zulu an' Burmese;
  But the Fuzzy was the finest o' the lot.
We never got a ha'porth's change of 'im:
  'E squatted in the scrub an' 'ocked our 'orses,
'E cut our sentries up at *Suakim*,
  An' 'e played the cat an' banjo with our forces.
    So 'ere's *to* you, Fuzzy-Wuzzy,
                    at your 'ome in the Soudan;
      You're a pore benighted 'eathen
                    but a first-class fightin' man;
      We gives you your certificate,
                    an' if you want it signed
      We'll come an' 'ave a romp with you
                    whenever you're inclined.

We took our chanst among the Kyber 'ills,
  The Boers knocked us silly at a mile,
The Burman give us Irriwaddy chills,
  An' a Zulu *impi* dished us up in style:
But all we ever got from such as they
  Was pop to what the Fuzzy made us swaller;
We 'eld our bloomin' own, the papers say,
  But man for man the Fuzzy knocked us 'oller.

Then 'ere's *to* you, Fuzzy-Wuzzy,
                   an' the missis and the kid;
   Our orders was to break you,
                   an' of course we went an' did.
   We sloshed you with Martinis,
                   an' it wasn't 'ardly fair;
   But for all the odds agin' you, Fuzzy-Wuz,
                   you broke the square.

'E 'asn't got no papers of 'is own,
   'E 'asn't got no medals nor rewards,
So *we* must certify the skill 'e's shown
   In usin' of 'is long two-'anded swords:
When 'e's 'oppin' in an' out among the bush
   With 'is coffin-'eaded shield an' shovel-spear,
An 'appy day with Fuzzy on the rush
   Will last an 'ealthy Tommy for a year.
     So 'ere's *to* you, Fuzzy-Wuzzy,
                   an' your friends which are no more,
     If we 'adn't lost some messmates
                   we would 'elp you to deplore.
     But give an' take's the gospel,
                   an' we'll call the bargain fair,
     For if you 'ave lost more than us,
                   you crumpled up the square!

'E rushes at the smoke when we let drive,
    An', before we know, 'e's 'ackin' at our 'ead;
'E's all 'ot sand an' ginger when alive,
    An' 'e's generally shammin' when 'e's dead.
'E's a daisy, 'e's a ducky, 'e's a lamb!
    'E's a injia-rubber idiot on the spree,
'E's the on'y thing that doesn't give a damn
    For a Regiment o' British Infantree!
        So 'ere's *to* you, Fuzzy-Wuzzy,
                        at your 'ome in the Soudan;
        You're a pore benighted 'eathen
                        but a first-class fightin' man;
        An' 'ere's *to* you, Fuzzy-Wuzzy,
                        with your 'ayrick 'ead of 'air –
        You big black boundin' beggar –
                        for you broke a British square!

Beja people ('Fuzzy-Wuzzy') of the Sudan, c. 1920

BOOTS

INFANTRY COLUMNS

W<small>E'RE</small> foot – slog – slog – slog –
                              sloggin' over Africa –
Foot – foot – foot – foot – sloggin' over Africa –
(Boots – boots – boots – boots –
                              movin' up and down again!)
    There's no discharge in the war!

Seven – six – eleven – five –
                              nine-an'-twenty mile today –
Four – eleven – seventeen – thirty-two the day before –
(Boots – boots – boots – boots –
                              movin' up and down again!)
    There's no discharge in the war!

Don't – don't – don't – don't –
                              look at what's in front of you.
(Boots – boots – boots – boots –
                              movin' up an' down again);
Men – men – men – men –
                              men go mad with watchin' 'em,
    An' there's no discharge in the war!

Try – try – try – try – to think o' something different –
Oh – my – God – keep – me from goin' lunatic!
(Boots – boots – boots – boots –
                              movin' up an' down again!)
    There's no discharge in the war!

Count – count – count – count –
                    the bullets in the bandoliers.
If – your – eyes – drop – they will get atop o' you!
(Boots – boots – boots – boots –
                    movin' up and down again) –
    There's no discharge in the war!

We – can – stick – out – 'unger, thirst, an' weariness,
But – not – not – not – not the chronic sight of 'em –
Boots – boots – boots – boots –
                    movin' up an' down again,
    An' there's no discharge in the war!

'Tain't – so – bad – by – day because o' company,
But night – brings – long – strings –
                    o' forty thousand million
Boots – boots – boots – boots –
                    movin' up an' down again.
    There's no discharge in the war!

I – 'ave – marched – six – weeks in 'Ell an' certify
It – is – not – fire – devils, dark, or anything,
But boots – boots – boots – boots –
                    movin' up an' down again,
    An' there's no discharge in the war!

PUCK'S SONG

Enlarged from Puck of Pook's Hill

SEE you the ferny ride that steals
Into the oak-woods far?
O that was whence they hewed the keels
That rolled to Trafalgar.

And mark you where the ivy clings
To Bayham's mouldering walls?
O there we cast the stout railings
That stand around St Paul's.

See you the dimpled track that runs
All hollow through the wheat?
O that was where they hauled the guns
That smote King Philip's fleet.

(Out of the Weald, the secret Weald,
Men sent in ancient years
The horseshoes red at Flodden Field,
The arrows at Poitiers!)

See you our little mill that clacks,
So busy by the brook?
She has ground her corn and paid her tax
Ever since Domesday Book.

See you our stilly woods of oak,
And the dread ditch beside?
O that was where the Saxons broke
On the day that Harold died.

See you the windy levels spread
About the gates of Rye?
O that was where the Northmen fled,
When Alfred's ships came by.

See you our pastures wide and lone,
Where the red oxen browse?
O there was a City thronged and known,
Ere London boasted a house.

And see you, after rain, the trace
Of mound and ditch and wall?
O that was a Legion's camping-place,
When Caesar sailed from Gaul.

And see you marks that show and fade,
Like shadows on the Downs?
O they are the lines the Flint Men made,
To guard their wondrous towns.

Trackway and Camp and City lost,
Salt Marsh where now is corn –
Old Wars, old Peace, old Arts that cease,
And so was England born!

She is not any common Earth,
Water or wood or air,
But Merlin's Isle of Gramarye,
Where you and I will fare!

THE WAY THROUGH THE WOODS

THEY shut the road through the woods
 Seventy years ago.
Weather and rain have undone it again,
And now you would never know
There was once a road through the woods
Before they planted the trees.
It is underneath the coppice and heath
And the thin anemones.
Only the keeper sees
That, where the ring-dove broods,
And the badgers roll at ease,
There was once a road through the woods.

Yet, if you enter the woods
Of a summer evening late,
When the night-air cools on the trout-ringed pools
Where the otter whistles his mate,
(They fear not men in the woods,
Because they see so few.)
You will hear the beat of a horse's feet,
And the swish of a skirt in the dew,
Steadily cantering through
The misty solitudes,
As though they perfectly knew
The old lost road through the woods ...
But there is no road through the woods.

HARP SONG OF THE DANE WOMEN

WHAT is a woman that you forsake her,
   And the hearth-fire and the home-acre,
To go with the old grey Widow-maker?

She has no house to lay a guest in –
But one chill bed for all to rest in,
That the pale suns and the stray bergs nest in.

She has no strong white arms to fold you,
But the ten-times-fingering weed to hold you –
Out on the rocks where the tide has rolled you.

Yet, when the signs of summer thicken,
And the ice breaks, and the birch-buds quicken,
Yearly you turn from our side, and sicken –

Sicken again for the shouts and the slaughters.
You steal away to the lapping waters,
And look at your ship in her winter-quarters.

You forget our mirth, and talk at the tables,
The kine in the shed and the horse in the stables –
To pitch her sides and go over her cables.

Then you drive out where the storm-clouds swallow,
And the sound of your oar-blades, falling hollow,
Is all we have left through the months to follow.

Ah, what is Woman that you forsake her,
And the hearth-fire and the home-acre,
To go with the old grey Widow-maker?

THE FABULISTS

1914—18

WHEN all the world would keep a matter hid,
    Since Truth is seldom friend to any crowd,
Men write in fable, as old Aesop did,
    Jesting at that which none will name aloud.
And this they needs must do, or it will fall
Unless they please they are not heard at all.

When desperate Folly daily laboureth
    To work confusion upon all we have,
When diligent Sloth demandeth Freedom's death,
    And banded Fear commandeth Honour's grave –
Even in that certain hour before the fall,
Unless men please they are not heard at all.

Needs must all please, yet some not all for need,
    Needs must all toil, yet some not all for gain,
But that men taking pleasure may take heed,
    Whom present toil shall snatch from later pain.
Thus some have toiled, but their reward was small
Since, though they pleased, they were not heard at all.

This was the lock that lay upon our lips,
    This was the yoke that we have undergone.
Denying us all pleasant fellowships
    As in our time and generation.
Our pleasures unpursued age past recall,
And for our pains – we are not heard at all.

What man hears aught except the groaning guns?
    What man heeds aught save what each instant brings?
When each man's life all imaged life outruns,
    What man shall pleasure in imaginings?
So it hath fallen, as it was bound to fall,
We are not, nor we were not, heard at all.

THE LAW OF THE JUNGLE
'How Fear Came', The Second Jungle Book

Now this is the Law of the Jungle –
as old and as true as the sky;
And the Wolf that shall keep it may prosper,
but the Wolf that shall break it must die.

As the creeper that girdles the tree-trunk
the Law runneth forward and back –
For the strength of the Pack is the Wolf,
and the strength of the Wolf is the Pack.

Wash daily from nose-tip to tail-tip;
drink deeply, but never too deep;
And remember the night is for hunting,
and forget not the day is for sleep.

The Jackal may follow the Tiger,
but, Cub, when thy whiskers are grown,
Remember the Wolf is a hunter –
go forth and get food of thine own.

Keep peace with the Lords of the Jungle –
the Tiger, the Panther, the Bear;
And trouble not Hathi the Silent,
and mock not the Boar in his lair.

When Pack meets with Pack in the Jungle,
and neither will go from the trail,
Lie down till the leaders have spoken –
it may be fair words shall prevail.

When ye fight with a Wolf of the Pack,
                              ye must fight him alone and afar,
Lest others take part in the quarrel,
                              and the Pack be diminished by war.

The Lair of the Wolf is his refuge,
                              and where he has made him his home,
Not even the Head Wolf may enter,
                              not even the Council may come.

The Lair of the Wolf is his refuge,
                              but where he has digged it too plain,
The Council shall send him a message,
                              and so he shall change it again.

If ye kill before midnight, be silent,
                              and wake not the woods with your bay,
Lest ye frighten the deer from the crops,
                              and the brothers go empty away.

Ye may kill for yourselves, and your mates,
                              and your cubs as they need, and ye can;
But kill not for pleasure of killing,
                              and *seven times never kill Man*!

If ye plunder his Kill from a weaker,
                              devour not all in thy pride;
Pack-Right is the right of the meanest;
                              so leave him the head and the hide.

The Kill of the Pack is the meat of the Pack.
                              Ye must eat where it lies;
And no one may carry away of that meat to his lair,
                              or he dies.

The Kill of the Wolf is the meat of the Wolf.

> He may do what he will,

But, till he has given permission,

> the Pack may not eat of that Kill.

Cub-Right is the right of the Yearling.

> From all of his Pack he may claim

Full-gorge when the killer has eaten;

> and none may refuse him the same.

Lair-Right is the right of the Mother.

> From all of her year she may claim

One haunch of each kill for her litter;

> and none may deny her the same.

Cave-Right is the right of the Father –

> to hunt by himself for his own:

He is freed of all calls to the Pack;

> he is judged by the Council alone.

Because of his age and his cunning,

> because of his gripe and his paw,

In all that the Law leaveth open,

> the word of the Head Wolf is Law.

Now these are the Laws of the Jungle,

> *and many and mighty are they;*

But the head and the hoof of the Law

> *and the haunch and the hump is – Obey!*

DANE-GELD

IT is always a temptation to an armed and agile nation
To call upon a neighbour and to say: –
'We invaded you last night –
                        we are quite prepared to fight,
  Unless you pay us cash to go away.'

  And that is called asking for Dane-geld,
    And the people who ask it explain
  That you've only to pay 'em the Dane-geld
    And then you'll get rid of the Dane!

It is always a temptation to a rich and lazy nation,
  To puff and look important and to say: –
'Though we know we should defeat you,
                   we have not the time to meet you.
  We will therefore pay you cash to go away.'

  And that is called paying the Dane-geld;
    But we've proved it again and again,
  That if once you have paid him the Dane-geld
    You never get rid of the Dane.

It is wrong to put temptation in the path of any nation,
  For fear they should succumb and go astray;
So when you are requested to pay up or be molested,
  You will find it better policy to say: –

  'We never pay *any*-one Dane-geld,
    No matter how trifling the cost;
  For the end of that game is oppression and shame,
    And the nation that plays it is lost!'

THE CHANGELINGS

R.N.V.R.

'Sea Constables'

OR ever the battered liners sank
    With their passengers to the dark,
I was head of a Walworth Bank,
    And you were a grocer's clerk.

I was a dealer in stocks and shares,
    And you in butters and teas;
And we both abandoned our own affairs
    And took to the dreadful seas.

Wet and worry about our ways –
    Panic, onset, and flight –
Had us in charge for a thousand days
    And a thousand-year-long night.

We saw more than the nights could hide –
    More than the waves could keep –
And – certain faces over the side
    Which do not go from our sleep.

We were more tired than words can tell
    While the pied craft fled by,
And the swinging mounds of the Western swell
    Hoisted us Heavens-high ...

Now there is nothing – not even our rank –
    To witness what we have been;
And I am returned to my Walworth Bank,
    And you to your margarine!

HYMN OF THE TRIUMPHANT AIRMAN

Flying East to West at 1000 mph

O H, Long had we paltered
　　With bridle and girth
Ere those horses were haltered
　　That gave us the Earth —

Ere the Flame and the Fountain,
　　The Spark and the Wheel,
Sank Ocean and Mountain
　　Alike 'neath our keel.

But the Wind in her blowing,
　　The bird on the wind,
Made naught of our going,
　　And left us behind.

Till the gale was outdriven,
　　The gull overflown,
And there matched us in Heaven
　　The Sun-God alone.

He only the master
　　We leagued to o'erthrow,
He only the faster
　　And, therefore, our foe!

* * *

Light steals to uncurtain
    The dim-shaping skies
That arch and make certain
    Where he shall arise.

We lift to the onset.
    We challenge anew.
From sunrise to sunset,
    Apollo, pursue!

* * *

What ails thee, O Golden?
    Thy Chariot is still?
What Power has withholden
    The Way from the Will?

Lo, Hesper hath paled not,
    Nor darkness withdrawn.
The Hours have availed not
    To lead forth the Dawn!

Do they flinch from full trial,
    The Coursers of Day?
The shade on our dial
    Moves swifter than they!

We fleet, but thou stayest
  A God unreleased;
And still thou delayest
  Low down in the East –

A beacon faint-burning,
  A glare that decays
As the blasts of our spurning
  Blow backward its blaze.

The mid-noon grows colder,
  Night rushes to meet,
And the curve of Earth's shoulder
  Heaves up thy defeat.

Storm on at that portal,
  We have thee in prison!
Apollo, immortal,
  Thou hast not arisen!

If —

If you can keep your head when all about you
  Are losing theirs and blaming it on you,
If you can trust yourself when all men doubt you,
    But make allowance for their doubting too;
If you can wait and not be tired by waiting,
    Or being lied about, don't deal in lies,
Or being hated, don't give way to hating,
    And yet don't look too good, nor talk too wise:

If you can dream – and not make dreams your master,
    If you can think – and not make thoughts your aim;
If you can meet with Triumph and Disaster
    And treat those two impostors just the same;
If you can bear to hear the truth you've spoken
    Twisted by knaves to make a trap for fools,
Or watch the things you gave your life to, broken,
    And stoop and build 'em up with worn-out tools

If you can make one heap of all your winnings
    And risk it on one turn of pitch-and-toss,
And lose, and start again at your beginnings
    And never breathe a word about your loss;
If you can force your heart and nerve and sinew
    To serve your turn long after they are gone,
And so hold on when there is nothing in you
    Except the Will which says to them: 'Hold on!'

If you can talk with crowds and keep your virtue,
    Or walk with Kings – nor lose the common touch,
If neither foes nor loving friends can hurt you,
    If all men count with you, but none too much;
If you can fill the unforgiving minute
    With sixty seconds' worth of distance run,
Yours is the Earth and everything that's in it,
    And – which is more – you'll be a Man, my son!

J.M.W. Turner, 'The Cholmeley Sea Piece' (1796)

THE STORM CONE

THIS is the midnight – let no star
Delude us – dawn is very far.
This is the tempest long foretold –
Slow to make head but sure to hold.

Stand by! The lull 'twixt blast and blast
Signals the storm is near, not past;
And worse than present jeopardy
May our forlorn tomorrow be.

If we have cleared the expectant reef,
Let no man look for his relief.
Only the darkness hides the shape
Of further peril to escape.

It is decreed that we abide
The weight of gale against the tide
And those huge waves the outer main
Sends in to set us back again.

They fall and whelm. We strain to hear
The pulses of her labouring gear,
Till the deep throb beneath us proves,
After each shudder and check, she moves!

She moves, with all save purpose lost,
To make her offing from the coast;
But, till she fetches open sea,
Let no man deem that he is free!

SONG OF THE WISE CHILDREN

WHEN the darkened Fifties dip to the North,
   And frost and the fog divide the air,
And the day is dead at his breaking-forth,
   Sirs, it is bitter beneath the Bear!

Far to Southward they wheel and glance,
   The million molten spears of morn –
The spears of our deliverance
   That shine on the house where we were born.

Flying-fish about our bows,
   Flying sea-fires in our wake:
This is the road to our Father's House,
   Whither we go for our souls' sake!

We have forfeited our birthright,
   We have forsaken all things meet;
We have forgotten the look of light,
   We have forgotten the scent of heat.

They that walk with shaded brows,
   Year by year in a shining land,
They be men of our Father's House,
   They shall receive us and understand.

We shall go back by the boltless doors,
   To the life unaltered our childhood knew –
To the naked feet on the cool, dark floors,
   And the high-ceiled rooms
                              that the Trade blows through:

To the trumpet-flowers and the moon beyond,
  And the tree-toad's chorus drowning all –
And the lisp of the split banana-frond
  That talked us to sleep when we were small.

The wayside magic, the threshold spells,
  Shall soon undo what the North has done –
Because of the sights and the sounds and the smells
  That ran with our youth in the eye of the sun.

And Earth accepting shall ask no vows,
  Nor the Sea our love, nor our lover the Sky.
When we return to our Father's House
  Only the English shall wonder why!

THE APPEAL

IF I have given you delight
  By aught that I have done,
Let me lie quiet in that night
  Which shall be yours anon:

And for the little, little, span
  The dead are borne in mind,
Seek not to question other than
  The books I leave behind.

Index of First Lines

Kipling in his study in Vermont, *c.* 1895